Christina Bützer

The Long Way Home

Contemplations of Southern Sudanese Refugees in Uganda

LIT

Bibliographic information published by the Deutsche Nationalbibliothek
The Deutsche Nationalbibliothek lists this publication in the Deutsche Nationalbibliografie; detailed bibliographic data are available in the Internet at http://dnb.d-nb.de.

ISBN 978-3-8258-0992-8

A catalogue record for this book is available from the British Library

Auslieferung/Verlagskontakt:
Fresnostr. 2 48159 Münster
Tel. +49 (0)251–62 03 20 Fax +49 (0)251–23 19 72
e-Mail: lit@lit-verlag.de http://www.lit-verlag.de

Distributed in the UK by: Global Book Marketing, 99B Wallis Rd, London, E9 5LN
Phone: +44 (0) 20 8533 5800 – Fax: +44 (0) 1600 775 663
http://www.centralbooks.co.uk/acatalog/search.html

Distributed in North America by:

Transaction Publishers
New Brunswick (U.S.A.) and London (U.K.)

Transaction Publishers
Rutgers University
35 Berrue Circle
Piscataway, NJ 08854

Phone: +1 (732) 445 - 2280
Fax: + 1 (732) 445 - 3138
for orders (U. S. only):
toll free (888) 999 - 6778
e-mail:
orders@transactionspub.com

Christina Bützer

The Long Way Home

Spektrum

Berlin Series on Society, Economy and Politics in Developing Countries

edited by

PD Dr. Dr. Ulrich van der Heyden (Department of Theology, HU Berlin)
Prof. Dr. Volker Lühr (Institute of Latin American Studies, FU Berlin)
Dr. Ulrike Schultz (Institute of Sociology, FU Berlin)
Prof. Dr. Manfred Schulz (Institute of Sociology, FU Berlin)

Volume 98

LIT

Dedicated to my family
for their boundless and
unconditioned support

Executive Summary

This paper examines the context of movement decisions and future expectations of Southern Sudanese refugees in regard to the signing of the Comprehensive Peace Agreement between the Government of the Sudan and the SPLM/A. Based on extended field research in the Rhino Camp Settlement, Northern Uganda, findings below explore individual aspirations of refugees in this particular setting. Acknowledging an axis of decision making conditions in the Sudan as well as in Uganda are considered to have decisive impact. At this, emphasis is put on the individuality of each refugee, rejecting simplifications of refugee populations as homogenous groups. The findings raise questions regarding the extent to which official repatriation, diminished as mass movement, ensures the needs of refugees. It will be argued that international organisations and the host government do not fully cover refugees' individual needs in exile. The findings will provide comprehension of personal motives. It will be suggested that when looking into repatriation, a refugee should be considered as an individual and not as a component of a homogenous group. It will further be argued that the concerned governments and organisations are responsible for the well-being of the refugees who are obliged to them and who have become particularly vulnerable, after basic bonds with their national government were broken. They should therefore not abuse their authority, but provide refugees with detailed information and enable them to make movement decisions based on facts. Furthermore, they should respect and help to facilitate the decisions individuals have thought out.

To ensure durability of repatriation, economic, social, infrastructural and political needs have to be addressed and the entire region rehabilitated. The high conflict potential of a return influx as colossal as the one expected and the cruciality of reintegration and reconciliation have to be acknowledged and addressed. It will be argued that the opportunity has emerged to meet the recent UNHCR policy of "prevention as the solution".[1]

[1] Dixon-Fyle (1994), p. 25

Contents

Figures

Maps

Acronyms

ACP	Assistant Programme Coordinator
CPA	Comprehensive Peace Agreement
DED	Deutscher Entwicklungsdienst (German Development Service)
GoS	Government of the Sudan
GoSS	Government of the Southern Sudan
GoU	Government of Uganda
GTZ	Gesellschaft für technische Zusammenarbeit (German Technical Cooperation)
IDP	Internally displaced person
IGAD	Intergovernmental Authority on Development
IGADD	Intergovernmental Authority on Drought and Desertification
JEM	Justice and Equality Movement
JRS	Jesuit Refugee Service
LRA	Lord's Resistance Army
NCP	National Congress Party
NGO	Non-governmental organisation
NIF	National Islamic Front (became National Congress in 1989)
NSCC	New Sudan Council of Churches
OAU	Organisation of African Unity
OLS	Operation Lifeline Sudan
OPM	Office of Prime Minister
RCC	Revolutionary Command Council
RWC	Refugee Welfare Council
SAF	Sudanese Armed Forces
SSIM/A	South Sudan Independence Movement / Army (name adopted by the main faction of the SPLA-United in September 1994)
SPLM/A	Sudan People's Liberation Movement / Army
SPLA - Mainstream	Name temporarily adopted from 1993 to 1994 by the Garang led faction of the SPLA
SPLA - United	Name temporarily adopted by the Riek and Akol led breakaway faction of the SPLA
SSDF	South Sudan Defence Force
TPO	Transcultural Psycho-social Organisation
UPDF	Uganda People's Democratic Forces
UPE	Universal Primary Education

UN	United Nations
UNHCR	United Nations High Commission for Refugees
UNICEF	United Nations International Children and Education Fund
WNBF	West Nile Bank Front
WFP	World Food Programme

Abbreviations

A.D.	after Christ
B.C.	before Christ
cf.	confer to
ch.	chapter
ed.	editor
e.g.	for example
et al	and others
ff.	following
km	kilometre
p.	page
sq.km	square kilometre

I Introduction

1. The field of research and its relevance

More than two decades of devastating civil war[2] in the Sudan have displaced some 4 million Southern Sudanese and have driven more than 400.000 across the national border.[3] The largest concentration of refugees anywhere can be found in Northern Uganda.[4] Here they live either as self-settled refugees or in officially designated camps and settlements, waiting for repatriation to their homeland. With the signing of the Comprehensive Peace Agreement (CPA) between the Government of the Sudan (GoS) and the Sudan People's Liberation Movement / Army (SPLM/A) at the beginning of 2005, the war between the North and the South has formally come to an end. However, territorial fighting still continues as well as intimidation through Ugandan Lord's Resistance Army (LRA) fighters.[5] On top of this, various peace agreements have previously failed, allowing serious concerns about the credibility of the current one, the implementations of which were delaying from the beginning.[6] Not much time has passed since the Southern Sudan has been released from the war, as a consequence of which, living conditions remain harsh and the region suffers from underdevelopment. In spite of all this, after decades repatriation has finally become a true option, if not spontaneously, at least after a foreseeable period of time. Yet, too quickly voluntary repatriation is considered obvious, neglecting the complex reality of refugee life. Many refugees left the Sudan under traumatic conditions and have stayed in exile for decades. Others have never been to their supposed homeland. Because of these considerations the concept of a return home is being challenged. Additionally, refugees might have

---

[2] Without disregarding the other wars within the country, war in this paper refers to war between Northern and Southern Sudan.

[3] cf. UN News Service (18.05.2007)

[4] cf. UNHCR (27.03.2006)

[5] In July 2006 peace negotiations between the LRA and the GoU began in Juba hosted by the GoSS and mediated by Dr. Riek Machar (vice president of the GoSS). The agreement that LRA rebels would move into allocated camps was never fully met and the entire region has suffered from increased instabilities since. cf. Gordon and Vandewint (2007), p. 25 ff. (For more information on the LRA see chapter III 2.2.2)

[6] cf. Human Rights Watch (2006)

adjusted to a life in exile and a newly founded existence. Refugees are frequently and hastily referred to as a homogenous group, denying them their individual contexts and aspirations. This generalisation leaves them even more vulnerable than they are anyhow, lacking the protection and guidance of their national government. In accordance with this fact, repatriation is often simplified as mass movement. This condition demonstrates the necessity to provide differentiated material on refugees' aspirations and motives, in order to assess their individual needs. In this approach a refugee population is thus not understood as being a homogenous group. The refugee is considered in his[7] full meaning as an individual human being, while being part of a certain group. Here, the population of the Rhino Camp Settlement, Northern Uganda.

2. Methodology and objectives

When conducting research, certain questions have to be addressed in advance. In the beginning, the researcher has to decide upon the field of the research. Furthermore, the methodology has to be chosen accordingly. Different phenomena require different methodologies and different methodologies provide different possibilities. By using the refugee population in the Rhino Camp Settlement as a basis for this paper, it became clear that this was fairly uncharted territory with regard to research. Little was known about the situation and hardly any literature was available. Furthermore, the research population is of a completely different cultural background than the researcher herself. To meet these challenges a methodology was required, which allowed the development and adjustment of research instruments in the research process itself. Basically, exploration had to start from a grassroot level. The researcher identified the Grounded Theory as the suitable methodology and remained unbiased enough to grasp unpredictable phenomena. Yet, in course of the research an adjustment of methodology was undertaken and elements of the Qualitative Content Analysis included. In the context of the Grounded Theory the question of research is the determination of a certain phenomenon, which is sought to be explored. It contains an essential direction of interest and

[7] The masculine form is used throughout this paper to embrace males and females alike. Only when referring to the researcher, the female form is used.

provides a surveyable framework. However, it has to be created in a manner which allows the examination of relevant, yet unexplored phenomena, therefore requiring flexibility and width in order not to restrict the depth of exploration.[8]

At the end of March 2006, a tripartite agreement between the Governments of the Sudan and Uganda (GoU) as well as the United Nations High Commission on Refugees (UNHCR) was signed in Kampala. Thus, the legal framework needed to coordinate, manage and facilitate the voluntary repatriation of refugees was set. The agreement affects some 168,000 Sudanese in Uganda, of whom almost 30,000 registered straight away.[9] However, this does not necessarily mean that they will actually leave. Life in exile has been provided with a completely new outlook, leading to the question whether peace alone will be reason enough for refugees to repatriate or if additional incentives are of importance. At the time when this research was being conducted, the tripartite agreement had not yet been signed and refugees were still uncertain when repatriation would commence. Therefore the question of research reads as follows:

> How are refugees at the Rhino Camp Settlement, Northern Uganda, responding to the fact that peace has been concluded and repatriation is becoming an official option?

The following analysis is designated to explore this phenomenon, which does not only examine the context of movement decisions and decisive factors, but also embraces what refugees anticipate from the new area of peace in the Sudan. This course of analysis derives from the fact, that the Southern Sudan people have been intensely exposed to times of war, but only have limited experience of peace. They have been part of a short interlude of silence and subjected to broken agreements and their harsh consequences. It remains to be seen whether the CPA has succeeded in creating confidence among refugees that a peaceful and decent life in contemporary Sudan is possible and how they are able to cope with that.

---

[8] cf. Strauss and Corbin (1990), p. 36 ff.
[9] UNHCR (27.03.2006)

3. Structure

In order to understand the refugee context and decision making process, two spheres of causality have to be distinguished and interrelated: the home country and the host country. In the case of the Sudan, there are, on the one hand, memories, which may be nostalgic and traumatic at the same time. On the other hand, there is the possibility of a country at peace. In Uganda, refugees are obliged to conform to official structures, while still having their own wishes and desires. The structure of the presented work is dictated by these conditions, namely: history, the present and the future of the Sudan and refugee life and conditions in Uganda as well as the refugees' conceptions.

The first part of this work embraces the context of the home country. The second civil war is understood to be the trigger for refugees to have gone to Uganda. Yet, the tensions between the North and South have pre-dated that war for hundreds of years. To draw a realistic picture of the centuries long conflict and to understand the deep distrust between Southerners and Northerners, we have to go back to the first encounters between Arabs and Africans in the Sudan. Furthermore, the Sudan is not only viewed as the trigger for flight, but also as grantor of conditions for repatriation. Thus, the current situation and future perspectives must be taken into account to allow comprehension of the complexity of the decisions which refugees need to make.

The second part of the work carries on with the attempt to understand the situation individuals have entered when being turned into refugees. Different points of view are considered. The office of the United Nations High Commission on Refugees, as the lead international agency for refugees, will be portrayed in its function and policy. At present, the poorer countries host most of the world's refugees, while the developed regions such as Europe and North America host the least.[10] Ironically, most refugees are forced to flee from one developing country to another, seeking refuge in countries with similar political and economic instabilities. This problem being a condition all too true for the border region of the Southern Sudan and Northern Uganda,

[10] Harrel Bond and Leopold (1994), p. 18 ff.

will be addressed in general and within context. Furthermore, a critical review on refugee life and relations between donors and clients is provided. Taking into account former experiences, the repatriation induced after the Addis Ababa Agreement will be examined. Additionally, information on current perspectives for repatriation will be provided.

The third part of the work displays the process of conducting research. Before providing traceability, the field of research is described in all its details. The entire process from preparations to data collection and to evaluation will be presented. Strengths and weaknesses shall be uncovered alike, in order to provide a foundation for following projects.

The results of the research are presented in the fourth part of the work. The material has been examined in accordance with the question of research, outcomes of which are presented in thematic units.

The last part of the work concludes the research and brings the results together to a broad understanding of the refugee context. Furthermore, the methodology is critically reflected and its value for the research examined. The profound and detailed outcomes allow for some recommendations for future procedure.

II The Sudan, its political landscape and conflicts

1. Any struggle must be anchored in history

The Sudan presents a multi-ethnic society with religious, ideological, linguistic, regional, cultural and ethnic cleavages. Neither the North, nor the South can be viewed as homogenous entities and none of those criteria has the ability to create one national identity. The Sudanese Arabs are divided into many ethnic groups with clear cultural differences and dialectal variations. The term "Arab" rather corresponds to cultural characteristics such as language and religion, but in phylogenetic terms, a majority of these are descendents of the Nubians.[11] Only the aggregation of all diverse groups by the state elite into one category allows us to speak of an Arab majority in the country.[12] It can also be questioned, if, without the confrontation with the North, there would even be a South as a viable political entity since the South is constituted of an even less homogenous group of people.[13] In spite of this diversity, the country is politically and economically dominated by a riverain central elite. The South, East and West have traditionally been marginalized and to this day, intentions to preserve a strong centralized unitary state continue to dominate state politics.[14] For the purpose of this paper, the North-South conflict, although it takes up only a small piece in the mosaic of the Sudan's multi-contested political environment, is given priority. To fully capture the meaning of the current peace in the Sudan, the genesis of the war has to be assessed. As the deceased first president of the Southern Sudan, Dr. John Garang de Mabior, put it: "Any struggle must be anchored in history".[15] The positions of refugees towards their compatriots in the North and, furthermore, towards their compatritos in the South are embittered by distrust. Decades of rejection have resulted in harsh perceptions of one another. The following paragraphs attempt therefore to track down the root causes of the division.

---

[11] cf. Krieger (1999), p. 254
[12] cf. Harir (1994), p. 21
[13] cf. Deng (1995), p. 9
[14] cf. Harir (1994), p. 21 ff.
[15] John Garang (2002) in London. Quoted in: Johnson (2004), p. XIV

1.1 Evolvement of division: The occupation of our land

> Arab[16] was not originated in Sudan, so they came and when we welcomed them, they have occupied our land and they don't consider somebody's right. (64, male, Equatoria)[17]

Encounters between Arab merchants and Africans in the Sudan started thousands of years before Christ, when the Sudanese began trading ivory, gold, slaves and other commodities with the Middle East via Egypt. These immigrants settled among the indigenous population along the Nile and integrated themselves into society.[18] In 641-2 A.D. an Arab army invaded Nubia.[19] Up to this point the North was divided into independent kingships, which defined their own hinterland, from which they took manpower, wealth and food surpluses and on which they built their power.[20] Although these Arabs came by force and established a remote control over the country, the Sudan was left in relative peace, autonomy and independence. Nevertheless, their privileged position made them an appealing class for intermarriage with leading Sudanese families and their culture was more and more adopted by and into the local society. This development was strongly furthered by the fact that inheritance among the local ethnic groups was through the female while among the in-coming Arabs it was through the male line. Thus the immigrants retained the gained power.[21] With further penetration, the kingdoms and their culture were undermined and by the beginning of the sixteenth century most of the indigenous peoples of the North had embraced the Islamic faith and Arabic culture.[22]

Penetration into the South, alternatively, was much more difficult for Arab immigrants and less appealing. Natural barriers, a climate unsuitable for camel-breeding, the difficulties of living conditions particular for desert people, and the resistance of the warrior Nilotic groups

---

[16] Without intending to fuel common polarization, the term "Arab" is used through out the entire work, when deriving from refugees' statements. (cf. ch. V 3.1)

[17] All interviewee quotations are followed by an indication of age, gender and home region. Interviews, which were translated in different modes, have been modified from reported speech to direct speech.

[18] cf. Deng (1995), p. 9 also cf. Al-Rahim (1969), p.6

[19] cf. Arkell (1961), p. 186

[20] cf. Johnson (2004), p. 2

[21] cf. Aguda (1973), p. 179

[22] cf. Duany and Duany (2000), p. 170 ff.

discouraged incursion.[23] The merchants were interested in the material value of the blacks as slaves and therefore had no wish to integrate or islamise them, given that Islam prohibits the enslavement of Muslims.[24] The separation between the protected centres and the unprotected hinterlands increased. In 1820 joint Turkish-Egyptian forces, led by Muhammad Ali, who was seeking the extension of Egyptian power, invaded the Northern Sudan. During the following Turco-Egyptian rule, the Sudan was brought together under one central authority, with its seat being the riverain city of Khartoum. The movement of the centre of power to Khartoum strengthened the central region at the expenses of the peripheries. Their favourable geographic location facilitated the formation of a strong riverain merchant class and Southerners found themselves confronted with a much stronger opponent than ever before. The conquered areas in the Northern Sudan were exposed to new forms of taxation, which demanded even more slaves from the South. During these times up to two million Africans were forced into slavery. The Islam practised by the new rulers, however, was hardly recognized as such by the Northern Sudanese, who characterized them as foreign unbelievers.[25] The suffering created by the so-called Turkiyya resulted in a joint revolt by Northern and Southern Sudanese forces. In 1881 Mohammed Ahmed Ibn Abdallah declared himself to be the expected Mahdi, the saviour, who came to redeem the corrupt world.[26] The joint forces overthrew the Turco-Egyptian regime and the Mahdi with his Ansar-sect formed the new government.[27] The so-called Mahdiyya, although involving Southern and Northern forces in its rise, must not be misunderstood as early Sudanese nationalism. The Southerners wanted to liberate themselves from foreign oppression and did not fight for the causes of the Northerners. After victory was accomplished, racial attitudes in the North remained unchanged from the Turkiyya and the

---

[23] cf. Deng (1995), p. 10 also cf. Al-Rahim (1969), p. 7

[24] cf. Deng (2001), p. 14

[25] In Sudan, Islam was basically introduced through preachers of mystical Sufi-orders. Sufism, is a mystical-ascetic form of Islam, which other than orthodox Islam, encloses emotional religiousness. cf. Schimmel (1990), p. 109 ff. Thus, the Sudanese Islam is a syncretistic belief, embracing Islamic symbols and pre-Islamic cultural habits. cf. Krieger (1999), p. 253

[26] cf. Johnson (2004), p. 5 ff.

[27] The original Ansar gave the Prophet refuge in Medani after he fled from Mecca in 622 A.D. cf. Anderson (1999), p. 66

Mahdist state developed its own way of internal oppression. Slavery did not only return, but intensified. After the Mahdi's death in 1885, his successor, the Khalifa, continued the spread of Islam. The riverain Sudanese proceeded to view political power as their prerogative and largely closed off the peripheries. A much sharper line than ever before was drawn between the Islamic region the Dar al-Islam and the non-Islamic region the Dar al-Harab,[28] abode of peace and abode of war, thus justifying exploitation of the Southern regions through jihad, holy war against non-Muslims.[29] The Dinka refer to this period of suffering as "the time when the world was spoiled."[30]

1.2 The Anglo-Egyptian Condominium: Southern voices overheard

> When the British came, these Northerners they got access to education and some went to advanced level and even to university. And in Southern Sudan, there were few people who were educated and their voice was not heard. (33, male, Upper Nile)

Without unifying the North, nor enclosing the South, the Islamic state gave way to British conquest in 1898.[31] Though the origins of the division of the North and South Sudan pre-date the unequal legacy of the colonial system, the Anglo-Egyptian condominium amplified North-South disparities vehemently. As early as in the 1920s, the Closed District Ordinance largely closed off the Southern provinces to Northern contact.[32] In 1930 the British released a "Southern Policy"[33], which declared that the administration of the South was to be developed along African rather than Arab lines. The colonial administration invested mostly in the economy, infrastructure and social services of the central region and least in the peripheries. The South therefore remained isolated and underdeveloped. With the British policy, claims for an independent South, even by means of violence, developed.[34] The administration system allowed riverain merchants, religious lead-

[28] cf. Schimmel (1990), p. 61 ff.
[29] cf. Johnson (2004), p. 6
[30] Ryle (1982), p. 28 (own translation)
[31] cf. Johnson (2004), p. 6 ff.
[32] cf. Johnson (2004), p. 12
[33] Johnson (2004), p. 11
[34] cf. Al-Rahim (1969), p. 8

ers and tribal notables in the Northern Sudan to accumulate rights to labour and land and therefore strengthened their power. In the course of this uneven development, education was a major vehicle. Political participation was discouraged in the South and the sensitive issue of education left in the hands of missionaries, who had other aims than creating bureaucrats or administrators.[35] According to Iten, in 1948 the same number of schools could be found in the Southern Sudan as twenty years before, namely 31 primary, two secondary and one trade school.[36] Particularly critical for the independent Sudan, was the development of two parallel elites in the country. Namely a christianised missionary educated elite in the South and a formally educated riverain elite in the North. The promotion of separation was intended to prevent economic integration of the two regions and by that thwarting any further spread of Arabism and Islam. Consequently, the two regions' cultural and religious identities grew in decisiveness. The separation left open the option whether to develop the South into a separate political entity or to integrate it into British East Africa. Then, only nine years before independence, amidst growing pressure from Egypt, the British reversed their policy of separate development. Yet, they had neither the time nor the political will to put in place arrangements that would ensure protection for the South in a united Sudan.[37] In consequence, the South lacked any real or potential influence on the country's political matters and all pledges for self-determination or postponement of independence were ignored.[38] In January 1956, independence was rapidly granted to the Sudan as a whole, even before the Sudanese government had agreed on a permanent constitution. Political power was exclusively transferred to the North.[39] The following Sudanisation – the process of replacing colonial administrators by nationals – was rather a Northernisation, as power was inherited by the heterogeneous riverain elite constituted of members from different families, clans, towns, Sufi-brotherhoods and socio-economic backgrounds. Of the eight hundred posts affected by the process, only six junior positions were granted to Southerners, leading to outrage in the South. However not only the South, but also the East and West

[35] cf. Tvedt (1994), p. 70 ff.
[36] cf. Iten (1983), p. 39
[37] cf. Deng (1995), p. 11
[38] cf. Johnson (2004), p. 11 ff. also cf. Tetzlaff (1992), p. 222
[39] cf. Johnson (2004), p. 29

were further marginalized. Hitherto, Sudanese nationalism is tantamount to the riverain elite's ideology of Islam and Arabism, who view the Sudan rather as an extension of the Islamic world, than as a national object of its own.[40]

2. The Anya Nya War (1955-1972): Patience has come to an end

> When I was in elementary school in 1968, I was in P4 when the Arabs where the ones ruling the Southern Sudan, they mistreat me very bad. I was having 12 lessons by Arabic teachers, (...) when an Arab thinks you are very clever, he is saying the very opposite that you are dull and promote someone other. That is why people decided to fight. (52, male, Equatoria)

Even before independence was granted in 1955, the absolute marginalisation of the South from the political, administrative and economic matters of the country led to the Torit mutiny, a two week long massacre in the province of Equatoria against Northern officers, administrators, merchants and their families. Suspecting a plot to murder them, Southern troops refused to transfer to Khartoum and instead defected with arms and ammunition.[41] In the course of the uprising 261 Northerners and 75 Southerners lost their lives; "the spiral of violence had once again begun."[42] In 1958, increased support from east and west Sudan for the South's pledge for a federal constitution prompted the military under General Abboud to take over.[43] Few, not even the large political parties themselves, mourned the passing of the coalition government.[44] With the aim to carry on Arabisation and Islamisation without democratic restrictions, party politics were outlawed. Abboud announced his politics in the slogan "a single language and a single religion for a single country"[45] and introduced forceful measures to promote nationalism throughout the country. A consequence of the artificial creation of a common identity through

[40] cf. Harir (1994), p. 21 ff.
[41] cf. Ali and Matthews (1999), p. 193 ff.
[42] Collins (1975), p. 67
[43] cf. Duany and Duany (2000), p. 175
[44] cf. Collins (1975), p. 71 ff.
[45] Assefa (1987), p. 58

suppression of ethnic diversity is decentralized violence against each other and against the state.[46] Instead of creating national unity under Islam, antagonisms were increased and the war was further fueled.[47] The following oppression forced thousands of Southerners either into the bush or into exile in Uganda, Kenya, Ethiopia and the Central African Republic. These refugees formed opposition organisations, pledging for self-determination and a peaceful solution. Meanwhile a military movement, mainly comprised of the Torit mutineers, emerged from the bush calling themselves Anya Nya – Snake Poison.[48] The objectives of the Anya Nya were clearly stated as follows:

> Our patience has come to an end and we are convinced that only use of force will bring a decision. ... From today onwards we shall take action ... for better or worse. ... We do not want mercy and we are not prepared to give it.[49]

The interests of both sides were all too obviously clashing and at the beginning of the 1960s a full-fledged civil war had developed.[50] The following massacres led to the displacement of hundreds of thousands of Southerners. Growing disenchantment with his politics, prompted Abboud to capitulate in October 1964. A caretaker civilian government took over, which gave reason to optimism and hope for a peaceful solution to the Southern problem. However, soon after, elections returned a coalition government that advocated a firm policy in dealing with the South. Large numbers of educated Southerners were killed or fled into exile and the will of Southerners to offer resistance stiffened.[51]

---

[46] cf. Harir (1994), p. 50 f.
[47] cf. Duany and Duany (2000), p. 173 ff.
[48] cf. Johnson (2004), p. 30 ff.
[49] Beshir (1975), p. 53
[50] cf. Deng (1994), p. 12
[51] cf. Beshir (1975), p. 81 ff.

3. Addis Ababa Peace Agreement: Neither Bible nor Quran

> There was a first agreement, which was in 1972 in Addis Ababa, and after all it was said that this agreement was not Bible or Quran and they changed everything, what they have said was gone, and we Southerners were surprised. (40, male, Bar al-Ghazal)

In October 1969, the Sudan came under military rule for the second time since independence. By announcing a different approach to the Southern conflict, solving it by political rather than military means, the new leader Colonel Jafaar Nimeiri again brought about short-lived hopes for reconciliation. Yet, soon Nimeiri was spending more than 40 percent of the state budget on war. These remarkable expenses, however, started to clash with his ambitions to turn the Sudan into the breadbasket of the Middle East, thus finally leading to another temporary change of policy.[52] Indeed, in 1972 the Addis Ababa Agreement induced a peaceful era. The agreement granted the South political and economic autonomy. But the Sudan's peace was short-lived, as the regime remained under pressure from the conservative and fundamentalist elements and, in particular, the sectarian parties and the Muslim Brotherhood.[53] Granting the South a degree of autonomy and democracy, which was not existent in any other part of the country, endangered the internal stability of the country.[54] Contrary, among Southerners the perception was predominant that the constitutional guarantees for autonomy were too weak and dissatisfaction with the failure of the central government to meet its financial obligations to the Southern region developed.[55] Furthermore, the sensitive border issue was never resolved and became intensified when oil was discovered. Discontent about water, the other main source of the South, escalated with the construction of the Jonglei Canal.[56] "As with oil, so with water: Khartoum proved itself to be more concerned with the extraction of the South's resources with the minimum return for the region itself",[57]

---

[52] cf. Tetzlaff (1992), p. 224 also Collins (2005), p. 36
[53] cf. Deng (1995), p. 12
[54] cf. Ali and Matthews (1999), p. 208
[55] cf. Akol (1994), p. 93
[56] In 1984 SPLA-attacks on canal and oil devices brought the projects to a halt. cf. Johnson (2004), p. 44 ff.
[57] Johnson (2004), p. 48

thus continuing with the traditional exploitation of the hinterlands. In 1978 the opponents of the Addis Abeba peace agreement regrouped and formed the Anya Nya II.[58] The South still failed to form one unit and divisions between leaders were exploited by Khartoum. By the early 1980s, "antagonisms within the South were as fierce as antipathy to the North".[59] Pressure for a review of the Addis Ababa Agreement and Islamic reforms of the legal system increased in the North and inspired the Presidential Decree Number One, which included the division of the South into three regions – the Upper Nile, Bahr al Ghazal, and Equatoria.[60] The order abrogated the Addis Ababa Agreement and returned power to the central government, "leaving three ghost regions in the South to masquerade as new institutions of regional self-government."[61] When the "September laws"[62] were introduced in 1983 and thus Sharia turned into state law, the Southerners' patience was overtaxed. As a result, the second civil war erupted and military conflict started anew.

---

[58] cf. Young (2005), p. 538

[59] Akol (1994), p. 93

[60] cf. Burr and Collins (1995), p. 15. Since 1994 these provinces have been divided into ten sub-provinces: Western Bahr al-Ghazal, Northern Bar al-Ghazal, Warab, Unity, Buheirat, Western Equatoria, Bahr al-Jabal, Eastern Equatoria, Jonglei and Upper Nile. cf. Krieger (1999), p. 256

[61] Alier (1992), p. 246

[62] Burr and Collins (1995), p. 15

4. The second civil war (1983-2005): Devastation of the South by the North and from within

The previous paragraphs have stressed the imbalance between the North and the South, which consequently led to the eruption of the first civil war. Opportunities to equalize the imbalance and to address the roots of the conflict were left unused. The unfulfilled promise of a "new deal"[63] reinforced frustration within the South and amplified hostilities. The second civil war has not only outmatched the first one in terms of atrocity but also the importance of ethnic dimensions of conflict has grown vehemently.[64] When in the following paragraphs the second civil war is analysed, it will become clear that civilians were the major victims of the conflict.

4.1 Creation of the SPLM/A: The vision of a new Sudan

With discontent over the division of the South and the introduction of Sharia law, armed Southern soldiers became a threat to the central government. However, Southerners refused to allow Nimeiri to disarm them and subsequently more than a thousand soldiers vanished into the bush with their weapons and ammunition. Here they started attacking enemy troops. Hence, Nimeiri decided to send one of his loyal Southern Colonels to negotiate with the mutineers, Dr. John Garang. Certainly, he had misjudged Garang, who did not attempt to appease the so called Anya Nya II fighters but defected with his entire force.[65] He succeeded in uniting major parts of the contested fighters in a single movement - the Sudan People's Liberation Army (SPLA) with its political wing, the Sudan People's Liberation Movement (SPLM).[66] The SPLM/A defined its objectives more broadly than any other Southern movement had before. As announced on SPLM/A radio, its ambition was

[63] Ali and Matthews (1999), p. 195
[64] cf. Krieger (1999), p. 324
[65] cf. Tetzlaff (1992), p. 228
[66] cf. Johnson (2004), p. 61 ff.

> to establish 'a new Sudan' of equality, of social and economic justice, where the various nationalities of the country can develop their cultures in freedom; where no particular religion is selected as the creed of the state; where there is recognition of and respect for human rights and where state power is not monopolized by a privileged few.[67]

Thus, the SPLM/A addressed underdevelopment and unequal development throughout the entire country. Still, independence always remained an unspoken option and there were parts of the group, who referred to talks of unity as merely tactics and separation as the true goal.[68] In fact, the notion of a New Sudan was quite appealing to Northern intellectuals and foreign supporters, but never found true resonance among Southerners. Still, with Ethiopian support, for which the call for a united Sudan was crucial, the newly formed SPLA largely defeated the separatist Anya Nya II rebels.[69] Yet, the SPLM/A was a fragile movement from the very beginning. Garang, Dinka by ethnicity, was highly educated but rather inexperienced in warfare and found himself challenged by the Anya Nya II for the leadership of the forces.[70] He was categorized as a "bookish young man whose head was full of theories, unrelated to realities of life in the forest and the countryside of the Southern Sudan."[71] Among traditional Dinka, academics were despised and frequently referred to as the origin of all troubles.[72] Consequently, factions detached themselves from the SPLA. For the actual conduct of the war on the ground Garang indeed had to rely on the support of more experienced veterans, such as his successor Salva Kirr Mayardit. As the conflict with the SPLA deteriorated into full-scale guerrilla war, the government had to come up with counter forces. Since the Sudan Armed Forces (SAF) were understaffed and mass induction encountered resistance among the Northerners, Nimeiri started arming irregular or militia forces.[73] Major parts of the war were thus carried out by proxy. Khartoum recruited, trained and armed Arab tribal groups supposedly against Southern rebels, but

---

[67] Alier (1991), p. 271
[68] cf. Johnson (2004), p. 65
[69] cf. Young (2005), p. 538
[70] cf. Burr and Collins (1995), p. 13
[71] Alier (1991), p. 261
[72] cf. Iten (1977), p. 208
[73] cf. Human Rights Watch (1990), p. 65 ff.

in fact unleashed them against their neighbours, particularly the Dinka.[74] In an exemplary fashion the massacre of El-Diein in 1987 illustrates, how neighbouring people were turned into deadly enemies, when more than 1000 Dinka were burned alive by Arab Rizeigats of the Baggara ethnic group.[75]
The SAF were above all involved in the defence of garrison towns, counter-insurgency activities and the retaking of garrison towns liberated by the SPLA, as well as the protection of road and river convoys. Their most durable legacy are the landmines which were planted around garrison towns to prevent civilians from leaving the army controlled areas. However, the SPLA itself also largely contributed to placing mines.[76] All warring parties ruthlessly targeted civil society. The use of strategies of scorched earth and starvation as weapons of war are most poignant examples.

4.2 Stubbornness of war

Although the roots of war in the Sudan have been laid out in detail, the reasons for the long continuation of several decades remain ambiguous. The conflict has survived every form of rule no matter whether it has been civilian or military. While the Northern regimes stubbornly blamed external forces for the war and degraded the conflict by scarcely labelling it as more than a local rebellion, the South declared the central government itself to be the problem, thus refusing to operate from within the structures of the political system.[77] After the coup d'etat of 1989, peace became more remote than ever before and large numbers of Southerners "followed the growing 'trail of [human] bones' eastwards"[78] to seek refuge in Ethiopia. Shortly after the coup, the SPLA fragmented into competing factions, thus playing into the hands of the willingly accepting North. It took more than one decade, for the SPLA to reunite and thus to stop hampering any potential peace attempt.

---

[74] cf. Deng (2001), p. 19
[75] cf. Tetzlaff (1992), p. 236 ff.
[76] cf. Human Rights Watch (1990), p. 67 ff.
[77] cf. Ali and Matthews (1999), p. 195 ff.
[78] Hutchinson (1996), p. 6

4.2.1 The diplomatic deadlock

In 1985, a popular rising in the streets of Khartoum, the so-called Intifada, prompted a Transitional Military Council under General Swar al Dahab taking over power, which the SPLM/A, however, denounced to "Nimeirism without Nimeiri".[79] The following period of democracy primarily failed to move towards peace because of the Prime Minister Sadiq al-Mahdi's "dithering and swithering",[80] who failed to address the major issues the country was facing. "Corruption, economic mismanagement and the continuing and rapid decay of state institutions were the dominant characteristics of the third democracy in the Sudan."[81] The coalition government behaved as if the Southern problem did not exist and resembled the previous two democracies in "ethnocentrism, political myopia and the self-righteousness typical of central riverain Islamic-Arabic elite."[82] Criticising his war strategy and insisting that he take serious measures to make peace, the army issued Sadiq al-Mahdi with an ultimatum. At the beginning of 1989 peace had almost come into reach, as negotiations for a ceasefire were running at full speed. A coalition joined by all parties except the fundamentalist National Islamic Front (NIF) was formed. Only the NIF insisted on maintenance of Sharia as state law, thus blocking any possibility for reconciliation with the SPLM/A. Its leader, Hassan al-Turabi, proclaimed a jihad against the Southern rebels in May 1989. The following month a group of committed Muslim officers, supported by the NIF, staged a coup and brought Umar Hassan Ahmad al-Bashir into power. The coup clearly intended to stop all negotiations with the SPLM/A and the peace process indeed came to an abrupt end.[83] The change in power increased Islamic fundamentalism. Under al-Bashir opposition was prohibited and the regime freed itself from most inner-political constraints. In fact al-Bashir appeared more eager to make war than peace.[84] Consequently, exile opposition was formed, with the creation of the National Democratic Alliance (NDA) coalition of the SPLA, major Northern political parties, armed groups and trade un-

[79] Khalid (1990), p. 353
[80] Khalid (1990), p. 355
[81] Harir (1994), p. 14
[82] Harir (1994), p. 16
[83] cf. Lesch (1998), p. 167
[84] cf. Burr and Collins (1995), p. 214

ions. Bashir's Revolutionary Command Council (RCC) of the Salvation Revolution held close relationships with the NIF. It advocated that Islam, as the religion of the majority and Arabic, as the language of the Quran, should found the country's nationalism and should therefore define the legal, political and economic system.[85] Since a majority of the fifteen officers of the RCC and members of the Council of Forty who advised the coup, did not provide the necessary conformity with this rigid ideology, they "soon disappeared from positions of authority at the same rate that members of the National Islamic Front acceded to power."[86] The stronger the South grew, the more Northerners felt threatened and the stronger their identification with Arab Islam grew.[87] In October 1993 the RCC transformed itself into a civil cabinet and the NIF took over. Al-Bashir was appointed president. During the following years would-be elections were held. Nonetheless, the reality was one of centralized control under a single ideology not leaving any space for negotiations with the SPLM/A or other marginalized areas.[88]

4.2.2 Playing into the hands of the government: A waste of time

> At first we were having one goal, the objective was only one objective, that to fight Arabs in Sudan. But in 94 I realized that there were some SPLA commanders who detached from the SPLA and they also fight against SPLA, which means that I decided that they were wasting our time. So it is better for me to leave them, the war, to come and seek refuge. (64, male, Bar al-Ghazal)

With the collapse of the Mengistu regime in Ethiopia in 1991, the SPLA lost its main supporter and large numbers of refugees were forced back to the battlefield, often haunted by bombs from the Bashir-regime. As the government did not allow food to be delivered to other places, relief efforts were concentrated around Nasir, near the Ethiopian border.[89] The chaotic situation resulted in a more urgent need for self-preservation than nationalism and thus, ethnicity became

[85] cf. Lesch (1998), p. 113 ff.
[86] Collins (1999), p. 106
[87] cf. Deng (2001), p. 19
[88] cf. Lesch (1998), p. 118 ff.
[89] cf. Johnson (1996), p. 176

a mayor factor to group around.[90] In the "process of privatising violence"[91] separate loyalties increased, while the over all control decreased. Personal enrichment became as important as the political agenda. The SPLA commanders of the region, Riek Machar and Lam Akol felt politically and militarily marginalised. The new relief situation gave them the opportunity to communicate directly with representatives of the UN and various governments. In actual fact, having weak operation structures, the Operation Lifeline Sudan (OLS) mission failed to implement its relief and development programmes consistently. The favouritism (and complete omission) of certain regions contributed to the SPLA split of 1991.[92] In August Riek and Akol announced Garang's overthrow. They condemned him as being a dictator, called for greater democracy within the SPLM/A and pledged themselves to a greater respect of human rights. They also declared the new objective of the SPLM/A being acquisition of independence of the South.[93] Since they did not succeed in overthrowing Garang, a major split erupted, which mainly ran along ethnic lines. Riek's SPLA-United was basically supported by Nuer, while Garang's SPLA-Mainstream was basically supported by Dinka. The two ethnic groups had been in conflict for a long time and cattle raids burdened relations between them. However, Dinka and Nuer had, being tied by similar customs, established a territorial balance.[94] But, when the SPLA split emerged, serious inter-factional fighting ensued, resulting in massive deaths and displacement of civilians.[95] The Khartoum government was highly satisfied by this development, as they could now blame tribalism for the destruction of the South. Furthermore, as Nyaba who was part of the Nasir coup himself, points out, "[i]t did not take long before the Nasir faction or its latter variations degenerated into the anarchy, autocracy, militarism, excessive human right violations, etc. against which the coup purportedly was staged."[96] The Southern Sudan Independence Movement / Army (SSIM/A), as it was called then, turned to the Khartoum government for weapons and ammunition to

---

[90] cf. Jok and Hutchinson (1999), p. 128
[91] UNHCR (1997), p. 25
[92] cf. Johnson (1994), p. 129 ff.
[93] cf. Johnson (2004) , p. 95 ff.
[94] cf. Iten (1977), p. 216
[95] cf. Petterson (2003), p. 64
[96] Nyaba (1997), p. 1

continue fighting against Garang. In 1997 Riek concluded a formal peace agreement with Khartoum, which he paid with a loss in credibility and civilian support.[97] The SSIA was officially transformed into the Southern Sudan Defence Forces (SSDF).[98] The liaison with Riek allowed the government to finally meet its long desired exploitation of the oilfields in the South and in 1999 a major pipeline became operational.[99] Meanwhile Garang encountered the revived NDA in Ansar, which welcomed him, being the commander of the only viable military force in opposition to the Islamists, in hope that he was going to bring forward democratization of the entire country.[100]

4.2.3 The military deadlock

> The SPLA was trying to maybe put something right, but many people they could not understand themselves, that is why they brought now corruption and division of the Southern region and between the people themselves. (50, female, Equatoria)

One has to wonder, why the Southern factions continued destroying their own entity, while actually sharing a common enemy. There was hardly any advancement at all and the factions were stuck in what Jok and Hutchinson call “the military deadlock”,[101] while the civilians themselves felt that their conflicts had always only been economic ones. They felt that the “nasty war”[102] was not theirs, but one which was forced upon them by the educated percentage of society. At the same time, although the South continued to weaken itself, the North did not manage to achieve a victory. For the South, the opposing factions had, in the past, been a joint force and therefore, knew perfectly well each other’s strategies, leading to a natural balance. Furthermore, both factions produced numerous splinter groups, which frequently turned to the Khartoum government and thus against the factions themselves. This is particularly true of Riek’s fragile SPLA-United. Khartoum was happy to support any splinter group willing to

[97] cf. Johnson (2004), p. 98
[98] cf. Jok and Hutchinson (1999), p. 129
[99] cf. Jok and Hutchinson (1999), p. 130
[100] cf. Colins (1999), p. 112
[101] Jok and Hutchinson (1999), p. 135
[102] Jok and Hutchinson (1999), p. 132

shoot in the process of destabilising the forces of both their enemy Garang and their alleged ally Riek. In fact, the central government had the aim of weakening all the major players and thus Riek's SSDF only received arms and ammunition, if they were to be used to fight against the SPLA. The SPLA alternatively, was well equipped because of help from various neighbouring African nations. It was the strong ethnic support for Riek instead, which prevented them from reasserting control in the Nuer regions of the Upper Nile. Although the government succeeded in subduing the Southern factions by making them incapable of action, it was part of the deadlock itself. Lacking broad knowledge of guerrilla methods, the army was unable to take ultimate advantage of the situation.[103]

5. The new area of peace in the Sudan

> We don't have any problems ourselves, if there are problems, they are all made by the Arabs. But the tribes, we have nothing against each other. (34, female, Equatoria)

5.1 Unity within the South: We have nothing against each other

In the year 1998, under the facilitation of the New Sudan Council of Churches (NSCC), Dinka and Nuer border chiefs finally entered into preparations for peace talks within the people-to-people peace strategy. The SPLA leaderships however, never seriously supported the negotiations, as they were in fear of a general fighting fatigue once the inner conflicts had been resolved. During the following months and years reconciliation meetings were held, with the Wunlit conference between Dinka and Nuer in March 1999 being the most significant one. Great success in settling tensions between various rival Southern Sudanese ethnic groups was achieved and a ceasefire between Dinka and Nuer was established. Apart from Garang, his successor Salva Kirr played a major role in these achievements. In December 1999, during a Nuer meeting in Waat, the formal break with the government and hence, with Riek was announced.[104] At the beginning of 2001, the SPLA entered talks with the Sudan People's Democratic Front - one of the largest Nuer political-military factions – and

[103] cf. Jok and Hutchinson (1999), p. 135 ff.
[104] cf. Johnson (2004), p. 125

succeeded in bringing serious attacks on the SPLA forces in the oil region to a halt.[105] In January 2002 Riek left Khartoum and the reconciliation between himself and Garang was finally announced. The symbolic implication was however, greater than any actual military benefits, since Riek, by then, had only few loyal troops remaining on his side. His legacy can be summed up in "the fomenting of civil war among the Nuer, and handing the oilfields over to the government".[106]

5.2 The Comprehensive Peace Agreement: A model for good governance in the Sudan

> The United Nations are to make sure that what they agreed in Naivasha is to be implemented, so that it will prevent war. And each part in Sudan or each region, like now you have heard that there is war in Dafur and there is war in eastern Sudan, also the Beja, they are demanding their rights and if their rights are not fulfilled, maybe it will also extend the fighting until it will include the others who have already got their right. (33, male, Upper Nile)

The war was accompanied by several peace attempts, initiated by various parties. Some agreements were closer to finding solutions than others, yet they were not co-ordinated and foiled each other. In 1992 and 1993, two conferences under the mediation of the then head of the OAU and president of Nigeria, Ibrahim Babangida, were staged in Abuja. However, in spite of competent personalities attending the latter one (including president al-Bashir), no earnest progress was made. With termination of Nigeria's responsibility as head of the OAU to attempt to resolve the conflict of the Sudan, the presidents of the north-east African countries perpetuated mediation. For this, they utilized the Intergovernmental Authority on Drought and Desertification (IGADD), chaired by president Moi of Kenya and including the presidents of Uganda, Ethiopia and Eritrea.[107] Four rounds of negotiation in the year of 1994 failed to solve the core issue of the relation-

---

105 cf. ICG, p. 142

106 Johnson (2004), p. 126

107 cf. Collins (1999), p. 113 f. The IGADD is the precursor of the IGAD and was founded in 1986. The IGAD functions as regional organisation of the Horn of Africa and embraces Ethiopia, Djibouti, Kenia, Uganda, Sudan, Somalia and since 1993 Eritrea. cf. Terlinden (2004), p. 1

ship between religion and the Sudanese state. Consequently, claims for self-determination grew louder. In 1997 Bashir finally signed a declaration of principles according to which territorial unity should only be given priority, if the Sudan formed a secular and democratic state. However, afterwards, Bashir quickly stated that the agreement was not legally binding.[108] It took until 2002 for the Intergovernmental Authority on Development (IGAD - as the IGADD is named since 1979) facilitated negotiations to accomplish a major breakthrough. With growing pressure from the United States the GoS and the SPLM/A resumed their negotiations and a framework peace settlement, the Protocol of Machakos, was signed and followed by a temporary ceasefire. The parties agreed upon giving unity priority, but also emphasised on the right of self-determination and a referendum on secession in the South in six years' time.[109] It further includes the acceptance of Sharia law in the North, a demand designed to give a measure of legitimacy to the ruling National Congress Party (NCP).[110] During the following years a series of agreements was signed under the auspices of the IGAD and, in respect to the issues related to the conflict areas of Southern Kordofan, the Blue Nile States and Abyei Area, under the auspices of the Government of the Republic of Kenya. The Government of the Sudan and the SPLM/A reached agreement on the aforementioned Machakos Protocol, the Agreement on Security Arrangements, the Agreement on Wealth Sharing, the Protocol on Power Sharing, the Protocol on the Resolution of the Conflict in Southern Kordofan and the Blue Nile States and the Protocol on the Resolution of the Conflict in the Abyei Area. The parties further concluded the Agreement on a Permanent Ceasefire and Security Arrangements Implementation Modalities and the Agreement on the Implementation Modalities of the Protocols and Agreements.[111] The Parties acknowledged

[108] Lesch (1999), p. 220 ff.
[109] IRIN News (2003)
[110] cf. Young (2005), p.535
[111] It cannot be the intention of this work to provide or analyze the details of these agreements. All of them can be found in the CPA itself.

> that the successful implementation of the CPA shall provide a model for good governance in the Sudan that will help create a solid basis to preserve peace and make unity attractive and therefore undertake to fully adhere to the letter and spirit of the CPA so as to guarantee lasting peace, security for all, justice and equality in the Sudan.[112]

On January 9th 2005 a ceremony was staged at Nairobi, where the CPA was signed by John Garang for the SPLM/A and vice president Ali Osman Taha for the NCF. Garang declared in his speech "Sudan for the first time will be a country voluntarily united in justice, honor and dignity for all its citizens regardless of their race – regardless of their religion – regardless of their gender."[113] Although the signing parties are obliged to the implementation of the CPA, the parties jointly requested international assistance. Garang was appointed first vice president of the Sudan and president of the Southern Sudan, while Bashir retained presidency and Taha became second vice president. The South is now fully independent of Northern interference, has its own army, its own resource base, access to oil revenues and control of its own branch of the National Bank. The South will be able to develop bilateral relations with international trade and development partners and ministerial power has been transferred to Southern representatives. The agreement gives the South religious autonomy and prevents the application of Sharia law to any non-Muslim throughout the entire country. After an interim period of six years, a referendum regarding secession from the Sudan will be staged, however, the CPA stipulates that unity be made an attractive option.[114] The formation of the new government was a major step forward in the implementation of the CPA. However, the key ministries of Energy and Mines, Defence, Interior, Finance and Justice were to remain with the National Congress Party, leading again to disappointment among Southerners. The hope remains, that the Addis Ababa dilemma will not repeat itself. The major weakness of the CPA is that it was only signed between two parties. As Human Rights Watch pointed out, "the NCP has the capacity to implement but lacks the political will, whereas the SPLA has the commitment but is weak and disorgan-

[112] GoS and SPLA (2005)
[113] IRIN News (2003)
[114] cf. Deng, Luka (2005), p. 7 ff.

ised."[115] Lacking functional party structures, the SPLM/A remains unable to successfully challenge the NCP on most issues relating to the implementation. The SPLM/A has failed to develop any viable civil, political and military institutions, basically due to Garang's attempt to maintain his hegemonic position in the SPLA and his fear that establishing strong systems of governance could lay the basis for a challenge to his authority. Thus, the SPLM/A has little experience and no model from which to operate.[116] To make matters worse, the Southern Sudan faces serious problems in meeting the new demand of educated people for the administration of the country,[117] since two generations are more or less without schooling.[118] Already from the very early stages on, implementations of the CPA were behind the plan.[119] Kumar further points out that war-torn societies tend to remain extremely polarised and extremist factions and warring parties constantly strive to undermine peace accords. He continues to say that the presence of large groups of ex-combatants pose a continual threat to a fragile peace.[120] Moreover, the exclusion of the many other groups in the country and the lack of broader support for the CPA, might threaten the long-term viability of the agreement.[121] With most of the government and state-resources being divided between the NCP and the SPLM/A, there was little to give to the large majority of Sudanese aside the agreement.[122] Furthermore, the CPA does not solve the other continuing conflicts in the country, most importantly in Darfur in the west and in the Beja region in the east. However, it could be taken as a model and the new power experienced by the SPLM/A could contribute to a general resolution. The pre-condition for a peaceful united Sudan lies in the recognition of the country's extreme diverse society and the provision of equal co-existence of all its components. If each group in society was granted relative autonomy and felt that it could develop its own agenda, entities might naturally move forward to a meeting place with the others.[123] Without inclusion of the

---

[115] Human Rights Watch (2006)
[116] cf. Young (2005), p. 538 ff.
[117] cf. Öhm (2006), p. 6
[118] cf. Breidlid (2006), p. 22
[119] cf. Human Rights Watch (2005)
[120] cf. Kumar (1997), p. 4 ff.
[121] cf. Baldo (2005), p. 25 ff. also Moszynski (2005), p. 17
[122] cf. Young (2005), p. 536
[123] cf. Simone (1994), p. 24 ff.

politically marginalised regions, however, the country might completely disintegrate.[124] The formation of one single Sudanese identity seems to be a great narrative, which collides with long-grown structures and concurs with the NCP's desire to ensure its own political survival. Indeed, one may believe that "reaching peace is (...) a degree easier than maintaining it".[125] Therefore, it remains to be seen, whether the North and the South are able to co-exist in one nation and whether the government in Khartoum, whatever its political philosophy, will ever accept the Southern Sudan as a partner in the Sudanese nation and genuinely share its power. If not, the South's request for secession is foreseeable. Yet, the response of the central government is unpredictable and secession would mean confrontation with the inborn heterogeneity of both North and South alike.[126]

5.3 John Garang's legacy

> There was real guarantee for the peace to succeed when the first vice president was in control. He knows the Arabs well and could deal with them according. Now that he is dead, I don't know what will happen. (38, female, Equatoria)

Only three weeks after he had been sworn in as vice president of the Sudan and as president of the Southern Sudan, Garang died in a helicopter crash on his way back from Uganda to the Sudan. Garang was succeeded by his deputy Salva Kirr Mayardit who now functions as the president of the Southern Sudan and vice president of the Sudan in his place. The sudden death of Garang weakened the SPLA however, the movement did not disintegrate.

Garang has been described as an intellectual with a vision,[127] "undoubtedly the only person who could articulate and reconcile the overwhelming desire for the South to peacefully secede with his vision of giving unity a chance during the six-year interim period."[128] Not only Southern Sudanese placed great hope and confidence into Garang. Many Northerners saw support to him as the best means to remove the unpopular NCP and bring about a democratic transformation in

---

[124] cf. Öhm (2006), p. 5
[125] Harir (1994), p. 58
[126] cf. Harir (1994), p. 61 ff.
[127] cf. Young (2005), p. 545 also Schmidinger (2006), p. 202
[128] Deng, Luka (2005), p. 15 ff.

the country.[129] Yet, as described above, his hegemonic, tribally stained legacy, has also weakened the SPLM/A structures and significantly decreased its capability to function as a viable government. Salva Kirr has only few of Garang's attributes. He is "not an intellectual, not urbane, has little understanding of the niceties of diplomacy, appears to have a limited interest in the rest of the country [...]"[130] and seems above all to aspire an independent South. Yet, he does also not share Garang's many failings and is said to follow a less tribalistic orientation. Indeed, one of his first acts of leadership was to confirm Riek Machar as his deputy. Riek being a Nuer might maintain unity within the South and reduce growing Dinka-Nuer tensions. Both, Salva Kirr and Riek, are said to be more open, transparent and comprehending in the system of governance decision-making and have better ties with Southern militias. With the new leadership being closer to the south Sudanese and the commanders in the field, there is a realistic chance for the SPLM/A becoming a more responsible organisation, developing an accountable leadership, and moving to overcome the current divisions of Southern communities. However, Salva Kirr being almost exclusively committed to the concerns of the South, does not nearly meet the great hope that was placed into Garang to contribute to the democratisation of the entire country and the resolution of the violent conflicts in Dafur and the Beja region.[131] Moreover, Garang as the founder and leader of the SPLM/A was seen as the saviour and liberator. It is questionable, whether any other person will be able to make his vision of a New Sudan alike appealing to the people of the Southern Sudan, as well as their compatriots in the North. His death has drawn into light the fragility of peace in the Sudan, as within few hours after the announcement of his death lootings and riots started in North and South alike. In Khartoum the largest numbers of rioters came from Dafur and the Nuba mountains, and to a lower extend from disadvantaged communities. Herewith, tensions between all of the Sudan's disparate peoples have increased, further undermining Garang's vision of a New Sudan and making fragmentation more likely.[132]

[129] cf. Young (2005), p. 535
[130] Young (2005), p. 545
[131] cf. Young (2005), p. 544 ff
[132] cf. Young (2005), p. 536 ff.

III The refugee context

The first sphere of causality, namely the history, the present situation and the future of the Sudan's contested political environment, has been elaborated in detail. Comprehensive understanding of the conditions, which forced refugees to flee their home country, has been provided, also an understanding of the current political situation. The following paragraphs will continue the discourse, by providing the context refugees entered into when they left their homeland. Hereby, the second sphere of causality will be addressed. Refugee life in general and in context will be examined and former repatriation as well as perspectives for future repatriation will be considered.

1. Refugeeism

1.1 The mandate and the clientele of UNHCR

The office of the United Nations High Commission on Refugees was established along with the Geneva Convention related to the Status of Refugees in 1951. It is mandated by the United Nations to lead and co-ordinate international action for the world-wide protection of refugees and to seek permanent solutions to the refugee problem. In the exercise of its function, UNHCR ensures that refugees and other beneficiaries are treated in accordance with internationally recognized standards and ensures that they are protected against forcible return.[133] According to the Geneva Convention mentioned above, the term refugee refers to a person who,

> owing to a well-founded fear of being persecuted for reasons of race, religion, nationality, or membership of a particular social group or political opinion, is outside the country of his nationality and is unable or, owing to such fear, is unwilling to avail himself of the protection of that country.[134]

[133] cf. Anand (1993), p. 53

[134] UNHCR (1997), p. 51

However, today refugees in the legal sense only constitute a little more than half of the people under the care of UNHCR. Other beneficiaries include internally displaced and war effected populations, asylum seekers, stateless people and others whose nationality is disputed, as well as returnees who, although they have returned to their country of origin, are still in need of support. Although the different groups of beneficiaries may differ considerably with regard to their individual circumstances and legal status, they all share a high level of human insecurity, most commonly due to the inability or unwillingness of their own state to protect them. The primary function of UNHCR is to compensate for this lack of national protection.[135] Traditionally UNHCR functioned as the main supplier of international aid. However, during the 1980s many donor governments started supporting the activities of their own national NGOs, expressing their lack of confidence in UN organisations. Thus UNHCR nowadays has to rely on NGOs for its resources and usually works with implementing partners.[136]

1.2 Refugeeism in Africa

With the wave of anti-colonial wars in the countries of the South a new set of forced migrants was unleashed who clearly deserved international protection, but yet were unable to prove individual persecution. Within the last decade, almost 40 percent of all martial conflicts of the world have taken and still take place in Africa.[137] Consequently, UNHCR's geographical reach, formally restricted to Europe, was expanded.[138] Furthermore, the term refugee was widened in the 1969 Convention governing the specific aspects of refugee problems in Africa.[139] The category refugee therefore refers not only to the persecuted, but also to

---

[135] cf. UNHCR (1997), p. X
[136] cf. Harrell-Bond and Voutira (1995), p. 214 ff.
[137] cf. BMZ (2004), p. 9
[138] cf. Barnett and Finnemore (2004), p. 90 ff.
[139] cf. Bakwesegah (1994), p. 6 also Harrell-Bond and Leopold (1994), p. 20 ff.

> every person who owing to external aggression, occupation, foreign domination or events seriously disturbing public order in either part or the whole of his country of origin or nationality, is compelled to leave his place of habitual residence in order to seek refuge in another place outside his country of origin or nationality.[140]

The majority of mass movements in the countries of the South are caused by war, ethnic strife and sharp socio-economic inequalities.[141] The Organisation of African Unity (OAU) definition consequently focuses on actual conditions inside the country rather than personal fear of persecution alone. Also, status is decided upon more by groups, rather than each person having to establish individual grounds for asylum.[142] However, by making geography a disqualifying factor, the masses of internally displaced persons (IDP), who are in refugee-like situations, are by definition still excluded: One has to cross a national border to be recognized as a refugee.[143]

1.3 A wider scope of responsibilities in poor host countries

Majority of the world's refugees are located in Africa, the Middle East, Southeast Asia and Central America. The poorer countries are hosting most of the refugees, while the developed regions such as Europe and North America host the fewest.[144] Ironically, most refugees are forced to flee from one developing country to another and seek refuge in countries with similar political and economic instabilities. The majority of refugees in the world today are women, children and handicapped people who often lack the mental and physical resources and strength required for survival under the harsh circumstances of forced relocation.[145] The UNHCR's formal mandate was to ensure the legal protection of those under its control without having the responsibility to ensure the physical welfare or even the survival of refugees. These duties lay with the host governments. With most of the host countries being as poor as the countries of origin and, therefore, often being unable to provide food, shelter, health care, or education even for

---

[140] UNHCR (1997), p. 52
[141] cf. Loescher (1992), p. 28
[142] cf. Harrell-Bond and Leopold (1994), p. 21 ff.
[143] cf. Bakwesegha (1995), p. 8
[144] cf. Harrel-Bond and Leopold (1994), p. 18 ff.
[145] cf. Marsella, Bornemann et al (1994) p. 2 ff.

their own population, the UNHCR had to step in. Consequently, the UNHCR has become increasingly involved in co-ordinating assistance, rather than only ensuring legal protection.[146]

1.4 Answers to the refugee problem

The recent UNHCR approach advocates "prevention as the solution".[147] However, the UNHCR's possibilities of intervening are very restricted. If refugee influxes cannot be prevented, there is an understanding between the above mentioned international convention of 1951 and the OAU convention of 1969 that the refugee status is temporary and durable solutions shall follow. A durable solution means the integration of refugees into a society. This is a political solution and depends on the political will, diplomacy, and statesmanship of governments.[148] It is anticipated that refugees will be repatriated and reintegrated into their home society, integrated into the host society or into a third country society after resettlement, in the very order of preference.[149] While voluntary repatriation seems to imply that the cause of flight has ceased, the latter solutions seem to be dictated by the acknowledgement of the fact, that the problems in the country of origin cannot be solved in foreseeable future.[150] The overwhelming size of contemporary refugee influxes makes permanent settlement a less tenable solution. In its beginning however, voluntary repatriation was merely an option, as the majority of refugees were fleeing from communist countries, and it was ideologically and politically unthinkable to send them back. Nowadays, as Stein points out, underdeveloped hosts and developed countries remain reluctant to permanently accept refugee populations for similar reasons. Both share concerns over costs in times of economic difficulty, doubts about assimilating those so culturally different, and believe that the numbers are too great to be absorbed. Donors frequently wish to reduce the costs for care and maintenance in exile, while at the same time wanting to keep refugees from their own countries, thus promoting local settlement or repatriation. The reception of refugees in Africa, particularly coming

[146] cf. Barnett and Finnemore (2004), p. 82 f.
[147] Dixon-Fyle (1994), p. 25
[148] cf. Stein (1986), p. 267 ff.
[149] cf. Anand (1993), p. 54 ff.
[150] cf. Zieck (1997), p. 3 ff.

from countries engaged in anti-colonial war, used to be viewed as an expression of solidarity.[151] By contrast, nowadays, the host countries' above stated concerns collide with the call for permanent settlement, leading to voluntary repatriation being the preferred durable solution. As no one is offering a true option for permanent settlement, the policy emerged, that if voluntary repatriation is not immediately feasible, it is sufficient to provide temporary settlement for refugees.[152]

1.4.1 Voluntary repatriation

Although officially being the most preferable durable solution in Africa, secure repatriation is usually the most difficult option to arrange.[153] As Coles explains, "a successful and relatively problem free return is more often the exception than the rule."[154] Voluntary repatriation is a misleading term. It neither officially entitles refugees to decide how long they may remain in exile, nor when to return. The change in the circumstances, which are crucial for the recognition as a refugee, legitimates the return to the country of origin. Six cessation clauses outline conditions, which release in principle both the country of refuge and UNHCR from their obligations towards refugees.[155] According to the rationale of the 1951 Convention, "international protection should cease whenever it is no longer either necessary or justified".[156] However, in practise, many asylum seekers are turned into "tolerated"[157] persons, who are not expelled once the decision on their non-eligibility has been finalized.[158] Indeed, the perception on when repatriation is possible and should be initiated differs significantly between concerned governments, the international community and the refugees themselves. However, it is the privilege of the home country and not the refugees, to change circumstances for the better. If this fails to be provided, refugees may be forced to remain in exile for decades.[159] It is possible that repatriation might be delayed due to the anxiety and

---

[151] cf. Rogge (1994), p. 18
[152] cf. Stein (1986), p. 264 ff.
[153] cf. Koehn (1995), p. 97
[154] Coles (1985) in Rogge (1994), p. 14
[155] cf. Zieck (1997), p. 31 ff.
[156] Kourula (1997), p. 118
[157] Rogge (1994), p. 15
[158] cf. Zieck (1997), p. 106
[159] cf. Bakwesegah (1995), p. 11 ff.

trepidation emanating from the refugees' themselves, who are often reluctant to return to their home country. That the return of refugees is natural and thus problem-free is "one of the most misleading myths surrounding the process of repatriation."[160] Sepulveda explains that evidence suggests that return may be more traumatic than the experience of flight and exile itself and even challenges repatriation as a desirable solution for the individual.[161] The repatriation process is often further complicated by the OAU's fundamental principle not to interfere with the internal affairs of other member states, thus undermining the political and humanitarian will of the host governments and all other agencies and organisations, to facilitate the refugees' safe return. In principle, UNHCR has no responsibility towards non-refugees and therefore towards their repatriation. However in practise, UNHCR usually assists them in returning home, yet, without the political will of both involved governments, UNHCR's and other agencies' ability to implement effective repatriation is limited. When large refugee populations are intended to be repatriated, certain requirements have to be fulfilled. As Bascom states "[r]epatriation may be the solution that suits 'external parties', but whether repatriation becomes a normative behavior or not largely depends on refugees themselves."[162] Needless to say, the underlying cause of the flight, such as armed conflict, has to be eliminated first of all. Desiring repatriation to be sustainable, a wider scope of issues has to be addressed, such as underdevelopment, democratisation, equality, justice, rule of law and human rights violations.[163] If repatriation is favoured, an environment has to be created, which allows refugees to return without risk and take up a normal and peaceful life. However, repatriations differ in terms of degree of voluntariness, levels of assistance provided, receptiveness to the returnees and their subsequent success in re-establishing themselves on their return.[164]

---

[160] Rogge (1994), p. 21
[161] cf. Sepulveda (1995), p. 83 ff.
[162] Bascom (1994), p. 227
[163] cf. Ziek (1997), p. 5 ff.
[164] cf. Rogge (1994), p. 29 ff.

1.4.2 Repatriation under duress

The principles of voluntary repatriation forbid any action, which obliges refugees to return to their country of origin, where their lives and liberty would be at risk.[165] In spite of all principles however, voluntariness of repatriation cannot always be granted. Repatriation under duress primarily occurs, when host governments, host communities or other actors behave in a way, which forces refugees to go back to their country of origin.[166] With increasing refugee populations and decreasing resources, the risk rises that refugees are pressured to return prematurely.[167] Coles notes that repatriations "have taken place when the underlying security or political problems had not been resolved fully with the result that the returns have not always proved durable."[168] The question emerges, how voluntary is voluntary? And when does it turn into a morally offensive dictate? Cases are known, in which, for example, refugees were told that food rations would be cut off if they did not repatriate.[169] As it will be pointed out below, on many occasions general conditions within a host country – i.e. social, political or economical –, force refugees, often together with the nationals, to either resettle or to forcibly repatriate. Refugee camps sometimes put refugees at a greater risk than the circumstances that triggered the original flight. Moreover, UNHCR itself frequently cannot prevent governments from denying refugees right of abode. At such times, it can only try to minimise the risk and make the best of a bad situation, even if that means contradiction with its own principles.[170]

---

[165] cf. UNHCR (1997), p. 68
[166] cf. UNHCR (1997), p. 147
[167] cf. Rogge (1994), p. 15 ff.
[168] Coles (1989) in Allen and Morsink (1994), p. 5
[169] cf. Stein (1986), p. 271
[170] cf. Barnett and Finnemore (2004), p. 93 ff.

1.4.3 Interim solution: Agricultural settlements

For reasons stated above, "often no durable solutions are at hand".[171] As repatriation is the most favourable solution to the refugee problem, programmes which aim at the permanent integration of refugees into the country of initial asylum have become rare. Instead temporary solutions, such as maintaining refugees on agricultural settlements where a certain degree of self-support is possible, are favoured.[172] Temporary however is a stretchable term, since some refugees remain in the settlements for decades. Harrel-Bond and Leopold argue that camps - settlement is considered a euphemistical term - constitute a health risk, take away the refugees' ability to control their own lives and generate hostilities among the local host population. Bagenda and Hovil believe that the settlement structure conspires against long-term development by disempowering refugees and thus perpetuating a cycle of paternalism. They continue to say that by taking away their individuality, the refugees' various backgrounds and potentials as well as their personal weaknesses are being neglected.[173] If refugees are obliged to stay in some kind of demarked areas, however, a settlement scheme can surely provide more self-dependence than a care-and-maintenance camp. Yet, crucial shortcomings remain. Although it has been widely accepted that assistance outside the camps is preferable, they still continue to exist. One reason why this is so is the bureaucratic need for accountability, which can best be served by keeping refugees in one place. The consequence, however, is the undermining of the refugees' autonomy and self-determination.[174] The donor community naturally searches for less budget demanding solutions. Relief, care and maintenance are expensive, but durable solutions of local settlement are expensive, too, especially when it involves development and infrastructural assistance. However, Stein argues, that refugee assistance should never be dominated by a balance sheet mentality, but is humanitarian assistance to restore victims of injustice to full membership in a human

[171] Stein (1986), p. 265
[172] cf. Rogge (1994), p. 20
[173] cf. Bagenda and Hovil (2003), p. 16 ff.
[174] cf. Harrell-Bond, Voutira et al (1992), p. 220

community. Thus, sometimes the right choice may be the expensive one.[175]

1.5 Relations between donors and clients

> We are in the hands of UNHCR. (34, female, Equatoria)

Givers and receivers in official refugee centres are, according to Harrel-Bond and Voutira, in competition over incompatible resources: The maintenance of authority, acquisition of material goods and independence.[176] The Terminology "givers" and "receivers" already displays the authors' positions. The existence of a refugee population is the pre-condition for any official assistance. Harrell-Bond argues that to maintain authority the refugee population and its dependence has to be preserved, which primarily serves the givers. Refugees would be able to administer and distribute the aid amongst themselves, such as happens in areas that are considered to be too insecure for humanitarian workers to enter.[177] The relationship between humanitarian workers and refugees is out of balance, as the latter are not able to reciprocate for the material aid given to them. Receiving a gift without being able to compensate leaves refugees with the feeling of obligation and inferiority.[178] They pay with their self-determination. This becomes particularly clear, when comparing official settlement to self-settlement which compensates refugees for the lack of donations by giving them increased socialisation, a greater sense of belonging and independence, as well as greater opportunities to generate income. Anticipating their role, refugees in official centres take up dependency themselves.[179] Having made it into exile in spite of harsh conditions, however, is an indication in itself that refugees are not as weak as sometimes assumed.

---

[175] cf. Stein (1983), p. 279 ff.
[176] cf. Harrell-Bond and Voutira (1995), p. 216
[177] cf. Harrell-Bond (2002), p. 57
[178] cf. Harrell-Bond (1999), p. 149
[179] cf. Ager (1999), p. 9

2. Refugeeism in the border region of the Sudan and Uganda

The research was conducted in the Rhino Camp Settlement in Arua District, Northern Uganda. The following paragraphs will provide background information on mutual refugee movements and the general situation of refugees in Northern Uganda. Uganda and the Sudan have a long history of cooperation and confrontation. Severe tensions developed when the two governments started arming rebel groups opposing each other.

2.1 The tradition of mutual border crossings

> So this is my third time now [to come to Uganda]. So we are now, these are our brothers and sisters. When there is wrong, I can come this way and when here is wrong, these brothers and sisters can even go and cross to us. (52, male, Equatoria)

As explicated above, there is a tendency for refugees crossing borders to replace one devastating situation with another. The case of the Southern Sudan and Northern Uganda cites as a prime example: Both areas have been affected by years of underdevelopment and conflict. Mutual border crossings therefore have a long tradition. Apart from this, both governments have supported rebel groups against each other, thus leaving relations in threads. As a result of the Mahdist revolt, the first wave of Sudanese migrated to Uganda as early as the end of the nineteenth century. Further groups of migrants seeking work arrived from the 1930s onwards. Most of them returned annually to the Sudan, but, after the eruption of the first civil war, remained in Uganda. They were joined by large groups of refugees fleeing martial conflicts.[180] Initially refugees settled along the border, but when Ugandan soldiers and Anya Nya rebels began fighting, they had to move more deeply into the country. Most of these refugees repatriated following the Addis Ababa Agreement. Those who remained behind, were basically compelled to flee along with Ugandan refugees in 1979, when the Ugandan president Idi Amin was overthrown by Tanzanian soldiers and Ugandan guerrillas. Amin had been very supportive to refugees due to a common ethnic background. After he was

[180] cf. Kabera (1987), p. 72 ff.

overthrown by Milton Obote, the peoples of the West Nile region and the entire North as well as the Sudanese were generally assumed to be supporters of Amin and thus became the main targets of military attacks.[181] As assaults continued, there were at least 300.000 Ugandan refugees accommodated in camps in the Southern Sudan under governmental and UNHCR supervision. After a change in government - Yoweri Museveni took over power in 1985 - some of these refugees repatriated voluntarily. Major numbers, however, were forced to repatriate later due to SPLA attacks. After the advent of Museveni, relations with the Sudan deteriorated. The main cause for this was the false assumption that Museveni had established close relations with Garang at the University of Dar-es-Salaam, thus alarming the government in Khartoum. In June 1987, Museveni visited Prime Minister Sadiq al-Mahdi in Khartoum and both sides agreed to no longer allow rebels to seek sanctuary in their territories. Despite the agreement both sides continued with their machinations and Sudanese troops even attacked targets in Northern Uganda. Several attempts to ease relations followed none of which accomplished any measure of success. The Khartoum government began its support for anti-Museveni movements as early as in 1986 and in 1992 started to provide support to the Lord Resistance Army and the West Nile Bank Front (WNBF), two Northern based movements. Only after his policy of non-interference had ultimately failed to produce results, Museveni started to support the SPLA in 1993.[182] In 1995 Kampala severed diplomatic relations with Khartoum. Meanwhile rebels continued to violate the Ugandan-Sudanese border. The war persisted, thus leading to continuous refugee crossings, while the Sudanese Air Force (SAF) repeatedly bombed Northern Ugandan towns, including refugee camps in Adjumani.[183] Both countries escalated their efforts to destabilise the other.[184] In consequence of the rebel attacks and the opening of key towns in the Southern Sudan, several thousands of Sudanese spontaneously repatriated in 1997. This movement was suspected to be influenced by the SPLA and their sympathisers. In the end large numbers of refugees hesitated and remained close to the border or even

---

[181] cf. Woodward (1988), p. 226 ff.
[182] cf. Prunier (2004), p. 363 ff.
[183] cf. Moro (2004), p. 425 ff.
[184] cf. Ofcansky (2000), p. 195 ff.

returned to their settlements. In May and June of 1997 UNHCR transported some 15,000 refugees back to the Rhino Camp Settlement.[185]

2.2 Current refugee accommodation in Northern Uganda

Sudanese refugees in Northern Uganda make up the largest concentration of Sudanese refugees anywhere and represent 80 percent of Uganda's total refugee population.[186] After intensified fighting in the Equatoria Province of the Sudan, more than 100,000 Sudanese fled to Uganda in 1993 - 1994 alone. These refugees were first of all accommodated in transit centres and later transferred to settlement schemes.[187] The larger number of refugees live in the three neighbouring districts of Arua, Moyo and Adjumani in the West Nile region, where in 2003 nearly 120,000 Southern Sudanese were settled. The underdeveloped North has always been the problem region of Uganda and these three districts are among the most poor in resource of the country. Their economy is based largely on subsistence agriculture, while still not producing significant food buffer stocks. At the same time the road and transport infrastructure is rather poor, employment opportunities in the formal sector are low and health indicators fall below national average.[188] The acceptance of refugees is favoured by the shared culture of the peoples along the border and encourages spontaneous settlement. The border line between the Sudan and Uganda actually separates single ethnic groups, as, for example, the Acholi, Madi and the Bari and Bari-related groups[189] and has hardly restricted human migration. Contrarily, increased nation building narrows the acceptance of refugees, in spite of ethnical, cultural, or political solidarities.[190] However, in the case of Uganda, the

---

[185] cf. Merkx (2002), p. 130 ff.
[186] cf. UNHCR (27.03.2006)
[187] cf. Merkx (2002), p. 128 ff.
[188] cf. Burnham, Rowley et al (2003), p. 54 ff.
[189] Tucker (1935), p. 885 f. divides the linguistic group of the Bari into the Bari (proper), the Pöjulu, the Kakwa, the Kuku, the Nyepu, the Nyangwara, the Mondari, and the Shir. Huntingford (1953), p. 26 ff. suggests a similar division, with including the Marshia, while not mentioning the Shir. According to Seligman and Seligman (1965), p. 239 the physique of the Bari-speakers differs to an extent, that the Bari-element is to be attributed to the assumption of language and culture, rather than genetics. Although their language is similar, there has historically been a degree of distrust between the groups. cf. Payne (1998), p. 60
[190] cf. Stein (1986), p. 275

North is still isolated from the centre and identification is low. Cross border trade has for a long time functioned as a substitute in order to make up for the lack of relations with the centre for both, Northern Uganda and the Southern Sudan.[191] As Woodward suggests when looking into the border region, "the surprise should not be that one makes connections between Northern Uganda and Southern Sudan, but that they were ever disconnected in the first place".[192] Loescher, alternatively, argues that, in particular, the common background of peoples can lead to intense hostility, as they can better and more quickly adjust themselves and thus appear as stronger competitors.[193] Needless to say, on top of that, integration always depends on the kind of refugee centre and government policies.

2.2.1 Settlement policy

In accordance with Ugandan policy stipulating that all refugees and asylum seekers must live in designated areas, the majority of refugees live in camps or settlements.[194] The opportunities offered in settlements have given Uganda the reputation of being one of the most generous host countries in Africa.[195] Refugees are allocated land for their private use, a practise which is not a matter of course in all African countries. Nonetheless, refugees are not landowners per se and, as Khasiani has pointed out, the areas allocated to refugees are most likely those, which are poor, unproductive and not claimed by nationals.[196] Although refugees have been encouraged to establish local councils, which allow them to voice their opinions to UNHCR, implementing programmes and local authorities, they do not have any official legal standing and refugees are denied the right to participate in local politics or to vote.[197] Merkx rates refugee settlement in Uganda as a great success, since it is becoming more and more difficult to distinguish refugees from nationals.[198] However, that does not meet the complex social structures stated above.

---

[191] cf. Merkx (2002), p. 122. ff. also Woodward (1988), p. 224 ff.
[192] Woodward (1988), p. 224
[193] cf. Loescher (1992), p. 48
[194] cf. Bagenda and Hovil (2003), p. 14 also Stein (1986), p. 275 ff.
[195] cf. Payne (1998), p. 1 also Burnham, Rowley et al (2003), p. 56
[196] cf. Khasian (1990), p. 372
[197] cf. Burnham, Rowley et al (2003), p. 56
[198] cf. Merkx (2002), p. 132

2.2.2 Security threats

The policy of keeping refugees in groups leaves them as open targets for rebels in zones of conflict. Indeed, insecurity started to become a part of daily life among refugees and nationals in Northern Uganda, when, in 1996, the West Nile Bank Front started attacking local communities as well as refugee settlements in the West Nile region. Refugees moved away from their plots and demanded military protection, yet, the numbers of the Uganda People's Democratic Forces (UPDF) divisions remained low and scarcely managed to prevent rebel attacks. Simultaneous to the instabilities west of the Nile, areas east of the Nile were under attack by the LRA. The LRA is known for its inhuman and cruel attacks on civilians, as well as the abduction and sexual enslavement of children, and has a long tradition of using the Sudan as sanctuary.[199] Formerly supported by the Government of the Sudan, the LRA is an opponent to the SPLA[200] and accused of having displaced 1.5 million people in that region, among them large numbers of refugees.[201] In July 1996 a massacre took place in the Achol-Pii Settlement in the Pader district, resulting in the death of 106 Sudanese refugees. Due to this lack of protection, refugees started to flee the settlements and thus became displaced within the country of asylum.[202] About 7100 of these displaced refugees were relocated and settled in the Madi Okollo Settlement in the district of Arua in September 2003.[203] With reference to the Achol-Pii massacre, Bagenda and Hovil argue that fundamental human rights were violated, as refugees were forced to live in insecure regions. They accuse UNHCR and the Government of Uganda of having failed to protect the refugees.[204] Colville argues that countries offering asylum bear full responsibility for the physical safety of refugees, while the UNHCR and other agencies can only advise the governments. He continues to say that by holding refugees in border camps, governments help nourish insecurity, which is then blamed on the refugees.[205] In 2006, some 146 peo-

---

199 cf. Acker (2004), p. 335 ff.
200 cf. Acker (2004), p. 352
201 cf. IRIN News (30.03.2006)
202 cf. Merkx (2002), p. 130 ff.
203 cf. DED (2005)
204 cf. Bagenda and Hovil (2003), p. 16 ff.
205 cf. Colville (1994), p. 19 ff.

ple died each week in the Northern region of Uganda, due to rebel incursions.[206]

2.2.3 The Self-Reliance Strategy

In the refugee centres of Arua, Moyo and Adjumani social services which consist of health, education, agriculture extension, water, sanitation and community services, were provided through NGOs, primarily funded by UNHCR. Standards were usually high above those of the district services. Allowing access to the nationals promoted the entire region. With shrinking global funds, however, as well as the fact that the West Nile Region was no longer considered an emergency, UNHCR decided to phase out financing for refugee programmes in the region in 1998. The so called Self-Reliance Strategy, which outlines the handover of services to the local governments of each district, was consequently introduced by UNHCR and the Ugandan Office of Prime Minister (OPM) in 1999. The process intended to eliminate the existence of parallel service systems while, at the same time, giving UNHCR the opportunity to channel funds into more critical situations elsewhere. However, the social integration of refugees into the host society is not part of this strategy.[207]

2.3 Repatriation after the first civil war

> This has happened also at first war in Sudan. Sudanese who were in Uganda, when they went back, they have stayed for two years and there is no schools, even no good health centre, no water, and many of them also have died, because the medicine is not available, especially for those who are staying in the villages. (40, male, Bar al-Ghazal)

After the conclusion of the Addis Ababa Agreement the repatriation of refugees from Uganda and other countries was induced. However, many refugees were reluctant to repatriate, as people who had earlier returned to the Sudan had been persecuted and apprehensiveness about security and freedom from retaliations developed.[208] In doubt of

[206] cf. IRIN News (30.03.2006)
[207] cf. Burnham, Rowley et al (2003), p. 57 ff.
[208] cf. Rogge (1994), p. 25 ff.

the government's intentions an attitude of "wait and see"[209] developed. Furthermore, poor management and poor infrastructural conditions after the long period of war resulted in the delay and sometimes the damage of supplies in the Southern Sudan. Most returnees, therefore, quickly turned to farming as a means of survival. Inadequate state services, limited markets and ineffective or inappropriate international aid remained a problem in large parts of the Southern Sudan. Thus, most expectations following the Addis Abeba Agreement were not met. While large amounts of money were invested in schemes, such as the Jonglei Canal, little was done from which the local population could actually benefit. Rather, the returnees were left alone to resettle and rebuild a livelihood. As Akol suggests, the degree of individual success might be related to the experiences, skills and relations established in exile and, therefore, to the way refugees had settled. Also striking is his argument, that the manner in which displaced were reintegrated after the Addis Abeba Agreement, is jointly responsible for its failure. The basic Southern economy and the corresponding lack of employment possibilities increased competition for political and administrative positions between returnees, remainees and the Anya Nya.[210] A major indication for the destabilising effects is the call for a separate Equatoria Region by new returnees in 1979. After the downfall of Amin, as pointed out above, the last remaining refugees had to eventually leave Uganda and repatriate to the Sudan. Being highly educated, they anticipated senior level jobs. However, these positions were already occupied, partly by Dinka or other ethnic groups from Bar al-Ghazal and the Upper Nile, thus leading to feelings of aversion. This experience also indicates the long-term challenge of any repatriation exercise and shows that success should not be measured prematurely. The strength of tribalism in the South and the elite's political culture, obsessed with job-distribution, prompted an increasing emergence of a Dinka domination issue at the end of the 1970s, which has not ceased to this day.[211]

[209] Akol (1994), p. 81
[210] cf. Tvedt (1994), p. 70 ff.
[211] cf. Tvedt (1994), p. 70 ff.

2.4 Current perspectives for repatriation

A tripartite agreement between the Sudan, Uganda and the UNHCR has been signed in Kampala in the end of March 2006. This agreement sets the legal framework needed to coordinate, manage and facilitate the voluntary repatriation of official refugees who desire to return. The operation is lead by UNHCR.[212] Thus, repatriation has become an official option. However, insecurities remain and previously described contradictions between key players started immediately. (cf. Ch. III 1.4.1) While Sudan's minister of state for the interior described the Southern Sudan to be secure and encouraged refugees to return, Uganda's deputy premier and minister in charge of refugees, as well as the UNHCR operations director for the Sudan and Chad, expressed serious concerns on the same issue. Refugee influxes to Uganda continued and serious fighting in the Southern Sudan, as well as attacks on UNHCR offices, were reported.[213] Next to a solution to the LRA intimidations, numerous Sudanese militia groups need to be included into the peace and reconciliation process. Furthermore, landmines and unexploded ordnance, which pose a threat to human security, have to be removed.[214] In addition, the prolonged conflict has had serious impacts on the South's development, as the primary focus in the region has been the meeting of emergency needs rather than development and reconstruction. In many areas basic social services are limited or non-existent.[215] An increase in users through large scale repatriations will for example exceed the capacity of health services and water sources.[216] Issues such as land allocation and livelihood opportunities also pose serious challenges to sustainable return.[217] While Sudan's minister of state for the interior admitted to the refugees that "it was not yet a time of 'milk and honey' in Southern Sudan"[218] UNHCR faces serious problems to provide the needed budget in order to adequately support return and reintegration operations. Upon their arrival, refugees are supposed to receive repa-

[212] cf. UNHCR (27.03.2006)
[213] cf. IRIN News (28.03.2006)
[214] cf. UNHCR (2006)
[215] cf. UNHCR (2006)
[216] cf. IMU OCHA (2005), p. 8
[217] cf. UNHCR (2006)
[218] IRIN News (28.03.2006)

triation packages including blankets, sleeping mats or mattresses, plastic sheets, mosquito nets, jerry cans, kitchen sets, water buckets, soap and food from the World Food Programme (WFP) to help them create new livelihoods.[219] However, the shortage in budget has life-threatening effects, as for example the process of demining is slowed down, for which only limited financial resources have been allocated. Yet, UNHCR recognizes that demining is crucial to the safe and sustainable return of refugees and IDPs.[220] Without sincere international support, the repatriation of refugees to the Southern Sudan is unlikely to succeed and to become a durable solution.

[219] cf. UNHCR (27.03.2006)
[220] cf. UNHCR (03.04.2006)

IV Empirical approach of the research

The theoretic framework of the empiric approach has been provided. As hinted at before, the signing of the CPA is a major turning point within the entire context of Southern Sudanese refugees as repatriation is turned into a feasible option. Consequently, the research approaches the question of how refugees relate to the phenomenon of repatriation and which future expectations they are holding. To meet this challenge, informal semi-structured interviews have been conducted and supplemented by a questionnaire survey. In the following paragraphs details of the field and population of research are provided. The research procedure will be displayed and transparency granted. Strengths and weaknesses shall be uncovered alike, in order to provide new approaches for following projects. The results will be presented in a separate, consecutive, chapter.

1. The area of research: The Rhino Camp Settlement

Rhino Camp Settlement received its name from the nearby town called Rhino Camp. The enclosure of the term Camp is thus merely a coincidence. As the epithet suggests, the place is a settlement not a camp. Beyond pure maintenance, a settlement is sought to provide opportunities for refugees to become more independent by providing them chances to develop their own livelihoods and integrating them within the official structures and systems of the host population. However, as pointed out earlier, voluntary repatriation has become the preferable solution, prompting reluctance to make sustainable commitments to programmes like Rhino Camp Settlement. (cf. ch. III 1.4) Mainly, the protracted nature of the civil war led to UNHCR and the Government of Uganda considering more durable solutions for refugees in Uganda.[221] When approaching the settlement, there is nothing like a fence or an entrance gate and it is hardly possible to distinguish between villages inhabited by refugees and villages inhabited by nationals. All administrative zones have their own trading centres. Small

[221] cf. Payne (1998), p. 1 ff.

shops, cafes, churches and sport grounds can be found throughout the entire settlement.

1.1 Geographical indications of the settlement

Rhino Camp Settlement was established in 1992 and is located about 66 km east of Arua town. The area comprises about 225 sq. km. Arua district itself lies in the far northwest corner of Uganda, bordering with the Democratic Republic of Congo and the Sudan.

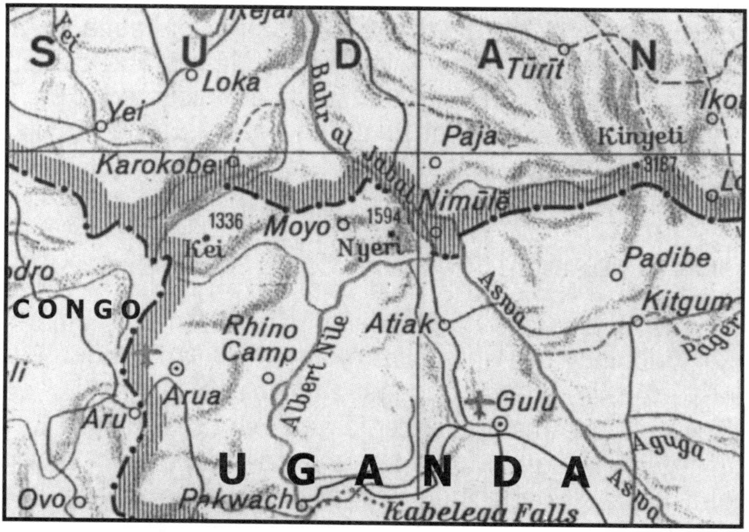

Map 1: Geographic location of the Rhino Camp Settlement

In accordance with the Government of Uganda, the land was made available to refugees by the local communities, represented through elders and local councils.[222] However, the environment has to be considered of low quality for human settlement. As Payne describes, the wider area "is a fairly barren land, with an unpredictable climate and rocky soils (...) [which] have always been essentially uninhabited bush, used by local chiefs for hunting deer."[223] She continues saying

[222] cf. Merkx (2002), p. 130
[223] Payne (1998), p. 9

that large parts were contaminated with tsetse flies before the refugees moved in and that scorpions and poisonous snakes are still common threats in daily life. "Poor soils, lack of water, few roads and the remote location have prevented all but a very small Ugandan population from inhabiting the area."[224]

1.2 Demographic indications of the settlement

By August 2004 the refugee population figure of Rhino Camp Settlement stood at 26,548 with a number of approximately 17,000 nationals living within the settlement boundaries and the immediate neighborhood.[225] Sudanese settled in Rhino Camp Settlement predominantly belong to the linguistic group of the Bari, with a majority of Kakwa, from Yei County of the Eastern Equatoria Province. The refugees are mostly of an agricultural background with some skilled artisans in mechanics, masonry, carpentry and tailoring, as well as civil servants. Thus, most of them rely on agriculture. Only few are engaged in small scale businesses or have found employment as teachers, in the health services or within NGOs.[226]

1.3 Formal settlement structures

1.3.1 Management structures

The German Development Service (DED) is the main implementing partner of UNHCR, both of whom have their offices in Arua town. The DED is in charge of camp management and has an additional office in the base camp of the settlement. DED is holding a separate contract with the World Food Programme (WFP) for management of the warehouses, provision of secondary transport and food distributions. In accordance with the Self-Reliance Strategy, the district of Arua through the relevant departments, is responsible for the implementation of activities in the sectors of education, forestry, community development, sanitation and health. The Office of Prime Minister, represented through a camp commander, is in charge of the legal matters of the refugees and security within the settlement. These institutions are supported by the Transcultural Psychosocial Organisation (TPO),

---

[224] Payne (1998), p. 9

[225] cf. DED (2005)a

[226] cf. DED (2005)

providing psychosocial counselling for traumatized people, the Jesuit Refugee Service (JRS), implementing peace education, Right to Play, coordinating and supporting sports activities and UNICEF, supporting the district with water and sanitation programmes in primary schools. As described previously, refugees in Uganda have been encouraged to form refugee councils. With that, the Refugee Welfare Council (RWC), which is based on the Ugandan local district council model, is representing the refugees. The settlement is divided into ten administrative zones, which constitute of 42 clusters.[227]

1.3.2 Official assistance structures

With the aim of phasing out dependency towards self-reliance, refugees are allocated plots of land, based on the number of household members, to cultivate their own food. Upon arrival they are provided with the necessities to start cultivation. Food rations are then gradually reduced, which leads to two caseloads: While refugees who arrived from January 2002 onwards receive the full ration, those who arrived before receive only 40 percent of it. Vulnerable groups, comprising physically disabled, single female-headed households with several children, single women, unaccompanied elders and unaccompanied minors, are treated with special consideration and are continuously granted full rations.[228]

1.3.3 Educational structures

There are fourteen primary schools and one secondary school (ordinary level) within the settlement.[229] According to the Universal Primary Education (UPE) approach of the Government of Uganda, primary school education is free of charge for nationals, while refugees have to pay a small administration fee. In 2005, a total number of 9,689 pupils have attended the educational services of the primary schools, with 5,508 being refugees and 4,181 being nationals. At 4,181, the number of girls is smaller than the number of boys at 5,231. The pupils are attended by 181 teachers, of whom 135 are refugees and 46

---

[227] cf. DED (2005)

[228] cf. DED (2005)

[229] The education system in Uganda is divided into seven years of primary school (P1-7) and six years of secondary school (S). The latter is subdivided into four years of ordinary (O) level and two years of advanced (A) level.

are nationals.[230] In addition, there is one vocational training centre offering skills training. However, access to these institutions is limited. While primary education is mostly affordable, secondary school is more expensive. According to the chairman of the Refugee Welfare Council, UNHCR provided only 13 scholarships for secondary schools in 2004.[231]

2. Preliminaries for the collection of data

2.1 Selection of methodology

The decision to enter an unfamiliar field of research strongly suggests the use of an explorative methodology. Furthermore, it was assumed that interview conduction was the most success-assuring instrument for research among the chosen population, rather than for example observation. This selection derives from the fact that statements on properties and facts were sought to be measured and not behaviour.[232] The literature suggests that qualitative interviews provide a high level of control over the survey process and a wide possibility to capture complex situations, which is important for an unfamiliar field of research, where exploration has to start at grassroot level.[233] The continuous alteration between conduction and interpretation, as suggested in the Grounded Theory, offered the most reasonable procedure to capture the yet unexplored field.[234] As it has been laid out before, the core of the research is the research unit itself. This concurs with the Grounded Theory referring to the question of research as the selection of a certain phenomenon, which ought to be examined.[235] In the process of interview conduction, however, friction emerged and therefore, the methodology was adapted. From formerly relying on the Grounded Theory alone, elements of the Qualitative Content Analysis were enclosed. Major reason for this was a lack of time, particularly due to compulsory movement, owed to severe sickness of the researcher. Although data analysis was not completely abrogated, it

---

[230] cf. Education Section of Rhino Camp Settlement (2005)
[231] Personal correspondence with the RWCIII Mr. Amule (20.05.2005)
[232] cf. Kromrey (2006), p. 346 ff. and 358 ff.
[233] cf. Schäfer (1998), p. 216 ff.
[234] cf. Strübling (2004), p. 13 ff.
[235] cf. Strauss and Corbin (1990), p. 37 ff.

was relegated into the background by the need for data collection. Apart from that, it turned out that the exploration of a wider spectrum of themes was desired, than had been intended and facilitated by the Grounded Theory, which strongly recommends focusing on one core category only.[236] Also, for reasons described below (cf. ch. IV 4.1.1), in spite of previous doubts, a questionnaire survey was initiated. This venture of cross-examination or triangulation was undertaken on the condition that different instruments can supplement each other, as suggested in the Grounded Theory and Qualitative Content Analysis alike.[237]

2.2 Construction of research instruments

2.2.1 Interview guidelines

In accordance with the principles of the Grounded Theory, discovery is the crux of the presented research. When choosing an explorative approach, interview guidelines are not static, but indeed flexible, to avoid the exclusion of unpredictable phenomena. However, the conduction has to be started from a certain, temporary, focal point. Ahead of the actual conduction a group discussion, facilitated by the retired Refugee Welfare Council of the settlement, was staged. Only afterwards, with a greater sensibility and understanding of the research population, focal themes were drafted. Inspired by the problem-centred interview, informal semi-structured interviews were chosen as the instrument of research. This interview form leaves wide space for the exploration of unpredictable phenomena, as it allows the interviewee to narrate openly. Concomitantly, it guarantees a certain extend of control to the researcher, who takes an active role within the phase of narration.[238] The fusion of few narration restrictions for the interviewee and essential control by the researcher becomes particularly functional when working with interpreters, a transfer of control itself.[239] In the beginning interviews were relatively open, with only general indications of focal themes. The following thematic units were distinguished:

---

[236] cf. Strauss and Corbin (1996), p. 98 f.
[237] cf. Mayring (1993), p. 112 also cf. Strauss and Corbin (1996), p. 4
[238] cf. Mayring (1990), p. 44 ff.
[239] cf. Diekmann (2000), p. 443 ff.

- Life in the Sudan before the war
- Life in the Sudan during the war (flight stimulus)
- Departure and flight
- Life inside the Rhino Camp Settlement
- Repatriation plans
- Expectations on the individual future
- Expectations on the future of the Sudan

This is not stringently following the methodology of the Grounded Theory, which would more likely suggest to keep the first interviews strictly open-ended and unguided, as to allow all potential core categories to enter. Yet, enough space for narrations aside of the thematic units was left and thus the exploration hardly narrowed down. In the later interviews, more and more probe questions were developed, as to elaborate certain categories. All concepts have been identified by the interviewees themselves, meaning they have not been asked questions such as "Do you have sufficient access to water?" Related contributions emerged in response to questions such as "What do you like about life at the settlement?" (By formulating questions in a positive manner, it was intended to get away from the stigma of refugee life as pure suffering.) With interview guidelines being constantly modified according to the phase of research, no general set of interview guidelines exists. The last version of guidelines, however, can be found in the appendix.

Ahead of the interviews, biographic information was inquired. As it turned out to be difficult for participants to respond in the chronological order proposed by the thematic units, an ancillary technique was designed. Before the actual conduction of the interview, a timeline was drawn on paper which covered stations of life from birth up to the arrival at Rhino Camp Settlement. Like this, participants were assisted in organizing their memories, while at the same time providing a basis for the researcher to continue from. Misunderstandings, as for example the question, whether war meant the first or the second civil war, could be prevented by referring to the timeline and pointing out the stages in a visualized manner. The timeline proved itself sufficient to provide an easy entrance to the interview and also to assist the interviewer and her interviewees in keeping track of the numerous and complex stations of refugee lives. Such a timeline looked, as for example in the case of James Awatu,[240] approximately like this:

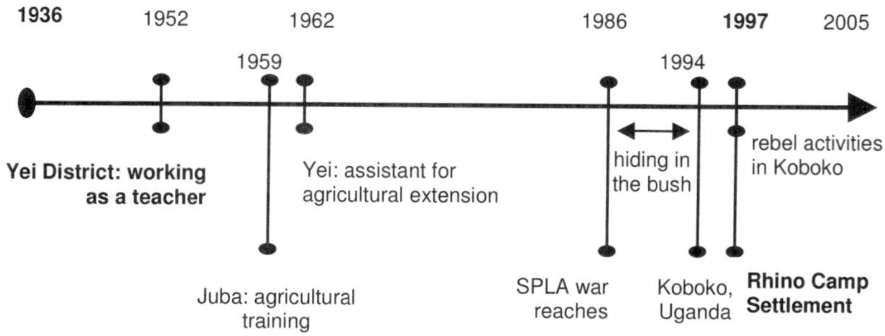

Figure 1: Example of a timeline

2.2.2 The questionnaire

The questionnaire survey primarily addressed a selection of categories, which yet lacked density, but nevertheless also elaborated new ones. Since the questionnaire was designed in the latter half of the expedition, the field of research had become more familiar and it was possible to produce an appropriate standardized measuring tool. The emphasis was laid on repatriation plans and preparations, as well as political assessment. For reasons of interpretation, background information was inquired into. A main purpose of the approach was to increase anonymity, particularly in regard to preparations in the Sudan. It is prohibited to cross the border without official permission and in the process of research, suspicion developed that participants hesitated to be frank about this sensitive issue. The introduction thus stressed the fact that responses could not be related to participants, intending to get unrestrained insights. Furthermore, admitting to having prepared a home in the Sudan, collides with a presumable desire to appear vulnerable to foreigners, who are associated with wealth and the donor community. That is why the identity of the researcher was kept concealed. Respondents were not manipulated in an unethi-

[240] All names, apart from those of officials, have been changed for reasons of anonymity

cal manner, as the introduction clearly stated the intention of the research, only that the origin of the researcher was not mentioned. The questionnaire combines open and closed questions and can be viewed in the appendix. The closed questions are of an ordinal manner and provided a selection of possible answers while the open questions are supplementative by asking for further explication and allowed free answers. The final questionnaire is based on the outcomes of a pretest.

3. Practical Preparations

First practical preparations for the research started as early as in the summer of 2003, when the researcher accessed the field of research for the first time. Upon arrival in 2005 permission from the National Council for Science and Technology in Kampala and its confirmation through the relevant Office of Prime Minister had to be acquired, in the case of refugee affairs the Department of Disaster Management and Refugees. Further clearance had to be purchased from the OPM, UNHCR and DED in Arua, as well as the camp commander of the settlement. Once inside the settlement, access to the research population had to be secured. Therefore, in order to guarantee the cooperation of cluster chairmen and refugees, the overall chairman of the Refugee Welfare Council had to be consulted. After his go-ahead he informed the zonal chairmen and requested their cooperation, these then passed on information to the cluster chairmen.

3.1 Recruitment of interpreters

Before being able to start with the data collection interpreters had to be hired. This was essential, as the research was not sought to limit itself to English speakers, who most likely have reached a higher level of education. Working with interpreters means having to rely on an external link between researcher and interviewee. As Khasiani points out "this is particularly problematic when using qualitative research methodology, where the effectiveness of the research depends on the ability of the researcher to notice and bring up interesting leads during the interview, then follow them through probing."[241] With the aim of

[241] Khasiani (1990), p. 373

avoiding a cultural gap, interpreters were recruited from the refugee population itself and required to speak various Sudanese languages, Arabic and English. They did not only translate whenever English was not useable, but also assisted in the organisation of interviews. For the questionnaire survey an additional interpreter was employed, who distributed questionnaires throughout the settlement, and also assisted in translation and writing in case of illiterate and non-English speaking refugees. The higher level of standardization restricted the influence of the interpreter, thus the questionnaire substituted the control usually kept with the researcher.

3.2 Selection of participants

With regard to formal settlement structures, the participants had to be identified through a cluster chairman or if not available his vice. Having to select through a middleman decreased the researcher's control of the selection process. The influence of chairmen was limited by letting each one appoint only two interviewees, leading to a more diverse and less subjective composition of the research unit. Furthermore, the chairmen were provided criterions that participants were required to fulfil. Therefore, as much control as possible remained with the researcher. Criterions were determined in the process of theoretical sampling, however, only to a limited extend. Theoretic Sampling means "sampling on the basis of concepts that have proven theoretical relevance to the evolving theory".[242] This implies, that in the beginning of the conduction the interest is to generate a possibly large and diverse number of categories, hence gathering a wide range of pertinent areas. In an advanced stage of the research, the focus is on development, density and saturation of categories, thus focusing on specific areas while intending to gain consistency. According to that the selection of participants is adjusted.[243] This kind of sampling requires interplay between conduction, analysis and participant selection, as well as advanced knowledge about potential interviewees. Initially, interviews were transcribed and analysed immediately and new participants chosen according to the outcomes. If a maximum of condensation of certain categories was expected, a follow-up interview was conducted. However, certain factors hampered this proce-

[242] Strauss and Corbin (1990), p. 177
[243] cf. Strauss and Corbin (1990), p. 176 ff.

dure. Most importantly, it was difficult to receive information about the participants in advance, who, as pointed out earlier, could not be selected directly. Moreover, aforementioned compulsory movements significantly decreased planning reliability which resulted in confusion with chairmen, participants and interpreters. A hasty and pressured atmosphere developed, which frequently did not facilitate the space for detailed examination of material necessary for the sampling.

In an attempt to grasp common experiences in the Sudan, the first participants were required to be of an age between 40 and 50. To provide a forum for comparison, first older, later younger participants (of both sexes) were selected. However, all interviewees were expected to be at least born after 1975 and having lived in the Sudan for considerable time. In the beginning, participants were required to plan to eventually repatriate to the Southern Sudan. Later on, a refugee was identified who intended to repatriate to Khartoum, in order to compare his specific context. Furthermore, while in the beginning participants were chosen regardless of their origins, leading to a clear Equatorian, Bari-speaking majority, later on Dinka from Upper Nile and Bar al-Ghazal were consulted to establish a new perspective of comparison. This strategy of identifying differences to provide comparison is referred to as "relational and variational sampling."[244] The respondents to questionnaires were not restricted through any exclusive factors. It was not possible and neither intended to provide a true random sample. Thus the arbitrary selection technique was deployed, which does not meet requirements of statistical probability calculations.[245] Consequently, it is not attempted, to draw conclusions for the entire refugee population of Rhino Camp Settlement.

[244] Strauss and Corbin (1990), p. 185
[245] cf. Kromrey (1998), p. 261 ff.

4. The data collection

4.1 The interview situation

Before each set of interviews permission from the according cluster chairmen had to be acquired. During these planning stages, interviews were scheduled and meeting points agreed upon. All interviews were conducted on a voluntary basis. In accordance with the opinion of the camp commander, no payment was given to interviewees at any time. As previously mentioned, only two interviewees were questioned from each cluster. Intending to create an atmosphere of privacy, chairmen were asked to provide a quiet and if possible closed place. The majority of interviews took place at community centres or at the homes of either the chairmen or the interviewees themselves. Exceptions were those interviews conducted outside Rhino Camp Settlement, which took place at private homes and offices within Yei town. Although the interpreters were trained to ask everybody not directly involved in the interview to leave the setting, chairmen often remained among the group and frequently other refugees could not be prevented from attendance. An interview situation is always an artificial situation as such,[246] but from the presence of the chairmen sometimes extra disturbance emerged. Another factor that might have influenced the interview situation is the presence of the SPLA inside the camp. Although the researcher could not witness any SPLA-presence inside the settlement herself, their presence has incontestable been reported by other authors.[247] De Lorenzo has pointed out that settlements in Northern Uganda are subject to regular visits by members of a network of SPLA intelligence operators. He notifies how the house of a refugee living in Miryei Settlement in Adjumani, who refused recruitment into the SPLA, has been burned twice. Furthermore, he reports how a young refugee, who had defected from the SPLA, had to be removed from Rhino Camp Settlement. There are chances that refugees' responds have been imbued by SPLA policy, for example relating to the question of repatriation, particularly when, with the attendance of a chairman, an authority was present. Notably in respect to the planned census in the Southern Sudan in the beginning of

[246] cf. Kromrey (2006), p. 360 ff.
[247] cf. Payne (1998), p. 63 also cf. De Lorenzo (1999), p. 24 ff.

2008, the SPLM/A has a strong interest in all refugees and IDPs returning to the South as soon as possible.[248]

4.1.1 Interviewee-researcher relations

It has been alluded for several times that some difficulties emerged in the interview situation. Although interpreters were trained to always point out that the researcher was an independent student, it is evident that she was frequently perceived as part of the donor community and a potential giver of financial assistance. Hence, the impression emerged that some participants manipulated their answers. One woman for example stated in the first interview that they lacked means to send her son to secondary school. Within a follow-up interview, however, it was revealed that the husband was employed as a watchman and paid the boy's fees. On other occasions, refugees directly asked the researcher for means to assist them, most commonly with school fees. Moreover, participants might have had an interest to transmit certain impressions to official institutions. The relationship between donors and refugees has been laid out in detail. (cf. ch. III 1.5) The decisive factor thus is how participants perceived the researcher, which may vary from individual to individual and does not have influence on all thematic units. The cross check outcomes of the questionnaire approach will be revealed in the evaluation process, although there is also no guarantee for them to be completely unbiased.

4.2 Material subject to evaluation

In Rhino Camp Settlement, 29 interviews with 27 individuals were conducted, which sum up to about 45 hours of conduction. To provide comparative material, four interviews were conducted in Yei, Equatoria Province in the Southern Sudan, with two Sudanese of the local community, who did not flee the country, the UNHCR Head of Field Office Ahmed Warsame, the Deputy Governor of Equatoria Johnson Juma and the Executive Director of Magwi Peter Otim. However, the question of research is concerned with the Rhino Camp Settlement population, and the purpose of all additional data is comparison and expert information only. Of the 20 questionnaires produced for the

---

[248] cf. IRIN News (20.06.2007)

pretest, 18 were returned. Of the 120 questionnaires produced for the actual conduction, 99 came back.[249]

4.3 Formal characteristics

All interviews, apart from those with officials, were recorded and later transcribed. As in most cases the words were delayed through translation, expressions and behaviour could not be interrelated and thus not considered. In those cases that were not recorded, a protocol was written. For the fluency of the text, interviews sometimes have been changed in person.

4.4 Composition of the research unit

According to the population figure of the settlement, the majority of the 27 interviewees are from Equatoria Province, particularly Yei district. Other Equatorian districts include: Kajo Kaji, Torit, Maridi, Juba and Magwi. Additionally two refugees from each province of Bar al-Ghazal and Upper Nile participated in the survey. The ethnicities vary on a wide range: 15 refugees belong to the group of Bari-speakers, with the majority being Kakwa and the rest being Bari, Kuku and Pöjulu. Others specified themselves as being Keriba, Latuka, Baka, Acholi, Luo[250] and Dinka. However some refugees simply defined their region of origin as their ethnic background. Slightly more males than females have been questioned, all from an age between about 33 and 65 years. The ages cannot be taken for granted, as many interviewees indicated that they did not know their exact date of birth. Ages were then estimated together with the interpreter. The ages of questionnaire respondents vary from about 21 to 58.

---

[249] The high response rate is due to the fact that questionnaires were not handed out to participants directly, but through an interviewer. When potential participants refused to respond, questionnaires were passed on to someone else. Therefore, the number of people having been addressed can not be estimated.

[250] Being from Wau, the participant most likely belongs to the group of the Jo Luo or Jur, as they are know to Arabic-speaking people and Europeans alike. cf. Butt (1964), p. 10 f. (Not to be confused with the Luo of Kenya.)

5. Process of data analysis

5.1 The interview material

In the analysis of the interview material, elements of two methods have been combined, namely of the Grounded Theory and the Qualitative Content Analysis. In the early stages of the research, when exploration had to emerge from the grass roots, the coding methods of the Grounded Theory clearly prevailed. That, in context of the Grounded Theory, analysis is integral to data collection has been laid out. Thus, first evaluations were already staged in the early phases of research to align the interview guidelines and to sample participants. With a serious loss of time and organisational difficulties, the constant alteration of data collection and data analysis could not be maintained. Thus, although analysis was continued to a lower extend, the better part had to be carried out after the data collection had already been concluded. For this, elements of the Qualitative Content Analysis were consulted. Qualitative Content Analysis defines itself as "an approach of empirical, methodological controlled analysis of texts within their context of communication, following content analytical rules and step by step models, without rash quantification."[251] To guarantee traceability, in the following paragraphs the process of analysis of the presented research will be portrayed.

In the context of the Grounded Theory, coding is the fundamental process of data analysis. All codes are developed in an inductive manner, meaning that each code is extrapolated from the material itself and not product of an external process of applying pre-knowledge. However inductive and deductive thinking form a fundamental interplay within the process. After identification of codes, they are rearranged, explicated and supplemented, including the application of external material. The first fundamental analytical approach of the Grounded Theory, with which the analysis was initiated, is the process of open coding. Open coding focuses on the identification and categorization of concepts. To do so, research material is divided into single entities and "conceptual labels [are] placed on discrete

[251] Mayring (2000, June)

happenings, events, and other instances of phenomena."[252] In the process, these concepts are constantly coordinated and grouped, like with like, as to reduce the number of units one has to work with. The resulting categories are "classification of concepts".[253] Moreover, properties and dimensions can be distinguished. Properties are "the characteristics or attributes of a category", while dimensions "represent locations of a property along a continuum."[254] Grounded Theory is a dynamic process which continuously validates its outcomes by taking them back into the material. The most elementary steps, such as data collection, can be continued up to the last stages of the research.[255] In the process of the subsequent two coding techniques, the axial coding and its continuation the selective coding, a central phenomenon, a so called core category emerges, around which all other categories are integrated. Material, not relating to this category, will no longer be considered.[256] In this research, these techniques have been initiated, but not stringently been followed through. Above all, no single core category has been identified, but several focal themes been addressed. For this purpose, processes suggested by the Qualitative Content Analysis were initiated. Two central procedures of the Qualitative Content Analysis are inductive category development and deductive category application.[257] As described above, the inductive category development has been initiated during the first stages of the research already and categories been coordinated, grouped and reduced. A coding agenda was arranged and, in preparation for the most central technique of the Qualitative Content Analysis, the structuring, each category was provided with a rule and represented by an anchor example.[258] The material has then been analyzed and scaled according to the rules. Core messages have been identified, which could be related to each other. The paradigmatic model, as the main instrument of the Grounded Theory to capture connections, was applied to the material. It reads as follows:

---

[252] Strauss and Corbin (1990), p. 61
[253] Strauss and Corbin (1990), p. 61
[254] Strauss and Corbin (1990), p. 69
[255] cf. Strauss and Corbin (1990), p. 17 ff.
[256] cf. Strauss and Corbin (1996), p. 98 ff.
[257] cf. Mayring (2000, June)
[258] cf. Mayring (2003), p. 82 ff.

causal conditions → **phenomenon** → context → intervening conditions → action / interaction strategies → consequences

Figure 2: Paradigmatic model[259]

Furthermore, in cases of passages requiring further explication, additional material has been consulted. This could be internal material, meaning the close context of a category within the data itself, or external material.[260]

5.2 The questionnaire material

The questionnaire is not understood as a consequently quantitative instrument, as questions were kept open in a qualitative manner, in order to maintain the explorative character of the research. It has been used to supplement and cross check the outcomes of the interviews. For that purpose, answers have been examined according to categories developed in the qualitative approach or in a separate deductive manner. For example, the interaction with staff members, some of them being refugees themselves, suggested that a number of refugees occasionally cross the border. The interviews did not reveal that. Therefore, the question "Since you became a refugee, did you ever go back to Sudan?" was designed. It was not only intended to densify categories, but also to find out if greater anonymity actually made a difference in respond patterns. A valuable insight from the questionnaire is certainly provided by the inductively developed categories on the effects of Garang's death. As no more interviews were conducted after the crucial date, questionnaires are the only references for implications of the sudden event for the research unit.

[259] cf. Strauss and Corbin (1990), p. 99
[260] cf. Mayring (2003), p. 77 ff.

5.3 Review

A main strength of the Grounded Theory is its flexibility. All outcomes are temporary and can be altered in the process of analysis. The data collection can be continued up to the very end of the research to supplement the rising theory and fill gaps identified in the process of analysis. However, as laid out before, a wider time frame than available in this research is required for the continuous interpretative work during the data collection. Additionally, the Grounded Theory seeks a profound understanding of one core phenomenon, which turned out to be too narrow as an intention for this particular research. By including elements of the Qualitative Content Analysis all inconsistencies have been tackled, and a comprehensive understanding of the research unit and related phenomena developed. Comprehension was strongly supported by actually living inside the settlement and constantly interacting with refugees and staff members. Extended stays and communication with refugees aside of the actual research itself, strongly contributed to the outcomes of the work. When it turned out that certain categories could not be elaborated on the interview material alone, questionnaires were used for further investigation.

Additionally, the research took advantage of explication strategies, by elaborating categories through either the material itself or through external material. Extensive literature review frequently helped providing information on categories, which could not be finalized with the material alone. All outcomes will be provided in the following chapter.

V Results of the research

In the following paragraphs the results of the research are presented. The question of how refugees cope with the fact that the peace agreement has been signed and repatriation is materializing into an official option is addressed. In that course, furthermore, refugees' anticipations of the new area of peace in the Sudan are considered. It has been argued before, that refugees are given limited space for decision-making. Uganda does not aspire to genuine integration and third country resettlement is even more unlikely. Consequently, only few options remain. One is repatriation, spontaneous or official, another one is prolonging the stay at Rhino Camp Settlement, which is merely a delay of repatriation. As no participant indicated any plan to repatriate spontaneously, repatriation in the following paragraphs is tantamount to official repatriation.

When intending to capture refugees' considerations, two spheres of causalities have to be distinguished: Firstly, circumstances and expectations of circumstances in the host country. Secondly, circumstances and expectations of circumstances in the homeland. Refugees are by definition forced to migrate into exile involuntarily. The voluntary nature of repatriation however, comes closer to general population movements.[261] Koser proposes that repatriation can be better understood, if repatriates are viewed as return migrants.[262] Migration concepts frequently refer to the push-pull model, which consists of the hypothesis that a combination of push-factors in the country of living and pull-factors in the country of migration influences the actual decision on whether to migrate or not. These factors consist of objective compelling and individual subjective impacts. Decisions are not only based on logical and rational expectations of advantages, but also on social and emotional bonds.[263] Although this model cannot be adopted one-to-one for repatriation movements, refugees are simultaneously pushed and pulled by certain factors, which can be rational or emotional. Factors are interrelated and in times cannot clearly be dif-

---

[261] cf. Bascom (1994), p. 227 ff.
[262] cf. Koser (1993), p. 173
[263] cf. Han (2000), p. 13 ff. also Treibel (1990), p. 29 ff.

ferentiated. The process of decision making starts out with an estimation of pros and cons for or against movement. Crucially, information has to be acquired first. Thus, the presentation of results starts out with the information system of refugees. The majority of participants indicated that they wanted to repatriate immediately, while only few are planning to remain. Various influences on the process of decision making have been identified, which will be presented in the following paragraphs.[264]

1. Foundation of decision making

The first individual of the research unit left the Sudan as early as 1987, the latest one in 1999. Only two interviewees indicated that they have been back to the Sudan meanwhile. However, the closeness to the border suggests that some might have crossed the border without authorisation, thus not mentioning their illegal behaviour. This suspicion is strongly supported by the fact that 17 percent of the questionnaire respondents indicated that they have been back to the Sudan since their flight. The majority described possibilities of gathering information about conditions in their home area through agents, such as people who are moving, even relatives who have travelled, letters from kin and radio broadcasts. Moreover, refugees who have returned are sending information about the current situation. One participant explained that he wants to observe first what is happening to those who return. Furthermore, several participants rely on UNHCR and trust that they will not start official repatriation, if conditions in the Sudan do not facilitate a secure staying. However, not all of them feel that they can rely on these sources and indicated that they have to return themselves to investigate the actual situation. Others negated having any ways of collecting information at all. The Deputy Governor of Equatoria and the Executive Director of Magwi explained that the SPLM/A would enter the settlements to "enlighten" refugees and encourage them to repatriate. At the time of conduction, however, they had not officially started doing so.[265]

---

[264] The provided results primarily emerged from the interview material. References to questionnaire outcomes are clearly indicated.

[265] Personal correspondence with Johnson Juma and Peter Otim (Yei, 29.07.2005)

2. Livelihood

2.1 Self-sufficiency and economic development

Not a single interviewee mentioned being unreservedly satisfied with life at the settlement. However few consider the abode endurable or even beneficial, such as

> I'm now having cloth. I can dress shoes, I can sleep on mattress, though I am a refugee, I have now my rights, I can go to church to pray. (...) So there is no problem, though there are some other things, which can make somebody very bad. (52, male, Equatoria)

Others do not see any alternative but to leave, making comments like

> for now the place in Yei is secure and in case there is going to be another war, that one will now go and get us there. Because the staying here, we are suffering too much, we are not able to tolerate any longer. (30, female, Equatoria)

Life is frequently described as a survival with nothing beyond. The most persistently voiced problem is poverty. Various aspects have influence on the process of decision-making. However, reaching the very basic needs of nourishment has priority above all other factors, not only with respect to quantity of mentions, but also in terms of intensity. The questionnaires however revealed that a number of respondents have well running businesses, which they are not willing to abandon yet. In case of the clear majority, the reasoning on the unendurable stay in the settlement starts out with the harsh weather conditions in the area. Participants indicate that no matter how much they dig, the harvests do not sustain them. As a result, refugees suffer from hunger. Since there are limited job opportunities, for most refugees the only possibility of generating an income would be selling their harvest. However, as plots cannot even yield enough for themselves to eat, there are no means of generating an income. The consequence is wide spread poverty. As it has been pointed out above, indeed the area and climate do not favour human settlement and agriculture. (cf. ch. IV 1.1) Obviously, the official assistance is not compensating for the restrictions imposed on refugees, who strongly feel changes through the introduction of the Self-Reliance Strategy.

> Before, when we came to Rhino Camp, the food UN was giving was a bit fair. In fact the food at that time, maybe a single person can get a basin at that time, compared to now, when now they are using maybe a saucepan which is half way cut, they cut that saucepan, they divide the saucepan into two. Now a person is supposed to eat that one for one month. (34, female, Equatoria)

Some go as far as accusing the agencies of being corrupt and not caring for them at all. Lado, who carried out research on agricultural land use in Maridi district (Equatoria), identified that as a result of long experience, peasant farmers have learned to adopt their methods of cultivation to the environment. Being placed in a different environment with deviate climatic and ecological conditions means loosing this advantage, which has been accumulated over generations.[266] Naturally, it is more difficult for refugees to cultivate in an unfamiliar environment. Bascom describes how self-settled refugees resettle in order to adjust to their kin driven "production systems".[267] By binding settlement refugees to an allocated piece of land and restricting their movement, these coping strategies vanish. Furthermore, foreigners applying for formal employment face restrictions on the issuing of working permits in Uganda.[268] Thus, it is no surprise that participants indicated that being in their home country alone will enable them to improve their living conditions, due to full citizen rights and familiar environments. The three Dinka who were interviewed all stressed on their particular situation as "someone who was not trained to dig or to cultivate"[269] and described difficulties to sustain themselves.

> Dinka are not used to dig with a hoe. We were cattle keepers and this causes a lot of problem to us. As you have seen we are not able to produce food for ourselves. Even anything to put into the market, there is no money, there is nothing. (36, female, Upper Nile)

---

[266] cf. Lado (1988), p. 25 ff.

[267] Porter (1987) in Bascom (1993)a, p. 323

[268] cf. Payne (1998), p. 125

[269] Quotations of interviewees in the text body that are rather used as key words to sum up a number of statements or reflect a common attitude, are not followed by a precise identification.

Dinka usually rely on a combination of livestock breeding and seasonal farming, which involves a lot of movement. Cattle are the foundation of the Dinka's livelihood and they are not used to sedentary life.[270] Thus, the lifestyle and the environment of the settlement, as well as the absence of cattle herds, are uncommon for Dinka who face extraordinary challenges in sustaining themselves. This is also true for others such as urban refugees. The contribution system per capita is obviously not able to address diverging conditions. Refugees are commonly referred to as a homogenous group and only especially vulnerable individuals are given specific consideration.

Consequently, participants expect to be able to bring about an economic improvement in the Sudan, albeit not without a period of adjustment and teething problems. Participants indicated that in the beginning they "will have nothing", but are going to "start from the scratch" and expect hardship in settling. Only two participants indicate to have relatives who have already constructed temporary houses for them and one expects to find his own house in Khartoum. The rest plan to leave with the entire family and then start construction, the same way as they had done before. The analysis of questionnaires produced a slightly different picture. Remarkably, seven questionnaire respondents indicated that they have already reconstructed their homes, a condition no interview participant admitted. It can be assumed that the latter were reluctant to lay open their own movement and development for reasons such as aid expectancy and prohibition of border crossings without official permission. A total of about 16 percent of questionnaire respondents indicated that their place has already been prepared either by themselves or relatives or alternatively their houses never collapsed. For the challenging period of transition, most participants hope for passage assistance from international organisations, but also from relatives, kin and the local community. Participants talked of "packages", which they expect to receive, same as it has happened during the repatriation after the first civil war.[271] The expected assistance includes most importantly food, but also tools, tents, jobs, money, loans, utensils, bicycles, fishing nets, mosquito nets, or even a plot to settle on. Participants indicated, that they are

[270] cf. Ryle (1982), p. 27 ff. also Iten (1977), p. 200 ff.
[271] cf. Merkx (2002), p.126

now in the hands of UNHCR and that they expect to continue receiving assistance,

> because if we go back, we will be like his kids. So like when your kid from somewhere comes home you are also to give something to that kid. (34, female, Equatoria)

They assume that after having catered for them for such a long time UNHCR will continue with that habit. Indeed, as has been laid out before, returnees belong to the group of UNHCR beneficiaries, who are not refugees in the literal sense (cf. ch. III 1.1) and UNHCR will facilitate their repatriation. However, the aspired composition of the packages does not exactly match the actual one, which has been mentioned before, (cf. ch. III 2.4) leading to the question to which extend givers bear responsibility for the appropriateness of their gift, which will be raised again below. (cf. ch. V 2.3) A minority does not trust UNHCR at all and suspects

> that if we will not open our eyes, this big big people of Yoro [the base camp] will just take us and pour us in the border and then we will go footing back to Sudan with no any help. (52, male, Equatoria)

Participants share the confidence that the favourable conditions for agriculture in the Sudan will not only enable them to sustain themselves but also to produce surpluses for commercial purposes. Others are expecting an employment or trust in the possibility to do their own small-scale business.

2.2 The ground to live on and cultivate

To meet aforementioned aspirations, returnees first of all need a ground to settle on and enough land to cultivate. A number of respondents are uncertain, whether they will be granted back the land they left behind. Others already received information that people have settled on their plots. Often the land left behind by refugees is appropriated by friends, relatives or others such as IDPs, who might be reluctant to hand it back to the original owners.[272] In fact, in the 1990s, when the fighting intensified in Equatoria, the SPLM/A did nothing to prevent Equatorians from moving into exile, and afterwards moved

[272] cf. Kumar (1997), p.17 ff.

large Dinka populations into the region, as to let them benefit from relief aid and protect them from severe fighting further north. Consequently, in 2005 there were still regions in Equatoria, where Dinka-IDPs outnumbered remaining non-Dinka by three to one.[273] The situation is further fuelled by the fact that much of the land is still not available for agricultural use because of landmines and other unexploded ordnance, same as running violent conflicts.[274] Nevertheless, interviewees display confidence in the new laws of the Southern Sudan, and trust that when they produce their papers of ownership, they will receive their land back. They further argue that peace will encourage those who might have settled on their ground to return to their own home areas. This concurs with the opinions of the Deputy Governor of Equatoria and the Executive Director of Magwi, who explained that there will be a judicial system to solve these problems and that every returnee has the right to prosecute his claim. They continue that those who occupy someone's land will be "enlightened" and that the width of the country will resolve the competition itself. However, settling in a different area will not always be an equally matched option for returnees, as land and ethnicity are often closely related to each other.[275] The two further share the opinion that returnees have to acknowledge that if it was not for the ones who liberated the country (instead of fleeing), their land would be occupied by the enemy instead,[276] an attitude also observed by Branch and Mampilly in Magwi county (Equatoria), where Dinka-IDPs indicated the date of when they have liberated the house above doorways.[277] The authors point out that the land distribution will be highly "tribalised",[278] as land disputes go to a body of elders and traditional leaders, who are likely to distribute land exclusively within their own ethnic group (thus excluding displaced Dinka from permanent settlement in Equatoria). Hereby, ethnicity will be further politicised bearing high conflict-potential.[279]

[273] cf. Branch and Mampilly (2005), p. 3 ff.
[274] cf. IRIN News (25.06.2007)
[275] cf. Rogge (1994), p. 39 ff.
[276] Personal correspondence with Johnson Juma and Peter Otim (Yei, 29.07.2005)
[277] cf. Branch and Mampilly (2005), p. 1
[278] Branch and Mampilly (2005), p. 12
[279] cf. Branch and Mampilly (2005), p. 10 ff.

2.3 Integration and reintegration

Participants do not feel properly involved in the official settlement administration and complain about heteronomy. They criticized the state of dependency they are forced to accept and feel that their concerns and questions are being disregarded. "We are under the care of UNHCR" was a common expression inside Rhino Camp Settlement and refugees often described UNHCR as being the "father and the mother of the refugees" in whose "hands they are". Others openly complained about heteronomy, such as "here people are just like you are in prison". Harrell-Bond and Voutira argue, that the familial idiom and the straight forward complaints, are describing the same relation between UNHCR and refugees, which has been laid out before, namely maintenance of authority on the one hand and acquisition of material goods and independence on the other. (cf. ch. III 1.5) The participants share the perception that as long as they are staying in the settlement, they are obliged to the UN. One indicated that they are expected to consume food, which they are not used to and which they neither know how to grow nor like to eat. Harrell-Bond has raised the question, if the giver bears any responsibility for the appropriateness or adequacy of the gift[280] and describes cases, in which refugees perceived inappropriate contents of food packages as disrespect.[281] A different participant described a lack of autonomy and its severe consequences as follows:

> I have now moved for different points, for many different points, started from Keri, Arua, Adjumani up to Rhino Camp, but what I am feeling bad about is just sickness. I feel really bad, because like Adjumani many people died there, because the place is densely populated. (...) So if I had not been in that point, I would have not got that sickness. So because I was now taken from this side to those ends, now I found that that place was densely populated, a lot of sickness, children die, hunger even, so that were only the things I felt bad. But actually because I am a refugee, I have no decision. I cannot make a decision that I am not going to such a place. So if UNHCR says you go this way, I can just move, I don't have now any alternative on that. (47, male, Equatoria)

---

280 cf. Harrell-Bond, Voutira et al (1992), p. 207

281 cf. Harrell-Bond (2002), p. 60

Obviously, participants feel that they are lacking self-determination. This becomes particularly true when it comes down to repatriation, about which they feel disregarded by the agencies. A woman in that course complained:

> I only wait to hear about going back to Sudan. When they had been taking the information here, that since two years ago, that we would be taken back and up to now we have not been taken back. From what I have known, we are treated like young children who when crying are given porridge so that they keep quiet. And up to now we are still waiting. (female, 65, Equatoria)

When talking to refugees the general impression emerged, that they were poorly informed about the process of official repatriation. Most of them were eager to acquire information on the process from the researcher, whom, being a European, they expected to be better informed. The poor and hardly existing communication between agencies and refugees underpins the refugees' feeling of being at UNHCR's mercy. Furthermore, Dinka interviewees even feel ethnically discriminated against by the settlement management, who according to them do not employ any Dinka at all due to their ethnic affiliation. Additionally to discontent with the official settlement structure, hostility between refugees and the local community occurs and, in times, also leads to economic disadvantages. Participants feel a gap between themselves and the nationals, for whom they frequently carry out casual labour or from whom they rent land. They complained about unfair behaviour after having cultivated on somebody's land or when their goats have encroached into nationals' fields and eaten their crops. As one participant explained,

> here, like where we are staying here, if we have animals like this, these people, the Lugbara here, they tend to pick those things away from us and the land, they grab away from us. (52, male, Equatoria)

The Lugbara are the largest ethnic group in West Nile and the predominant ethnic group among nationals living within the settlement boundaries. In spite of a shared historical and ethnic background with large parts of the refugee population,[282] participants feel alienated and relations are often dominated by tension. Strained relations are, how-

[282] cf. Shiroya (1972), p. 23 ff.

ever, not only restricted to relations with the nationals, but also occur between the different Southern Sudanese tribes. A Dinka woman described how she and her ethnic mates face problems, sometimes even violent, with refugees and nationals alike:

> Coming to a tribe like Dinka, we are minority in Rhino Camp and when you look at us, we don't have any other language apart from Dinka. People who happen to know other languages, it might be Arabic or English like that. But our culture is not the same with the local people here. Now even when I have a problem or someone apart from me has a problem with a national or any tribe here and there is nobody to connect us, to translate what I wanted to say, I will get stucked and those problems will also remain on my neck. Now here in the camp, when I have a problem with a neighbour or someone apart from Dinka, because the other tribes are majority, they can go to the police and bring the police and say this were the bad people in Sudan, they were soldiers, whatever. All this thing they can put on your neck and even when you tell your truth, nobody who can listen. Even the national or the policeman will not listen to you. All these problems I face here in Rhino Camp as a Dinka. (36, female, Upper Nile)

The Dinka refugees are left especially vulnerable, predicated on the highly politicized relations between them and other ethnic groups in the Southern Sudan before and during the war. Payne refers to "deep-felt prejudice and mistrust that stems from cultural and political differences between the Dinka and many other tribes of south Sudan",[283] a condition, according to Moro, never comprehended by the aid agencies, who again refer to refugees as "masses of desperate people in need of assistance."[284] In Rhino Camp Settlement Dinka are settled in separate clusters. In Adjumani hostilities went as far that Dinka were completely denied permanent settlement among other refugees.[285]
Furthermore, participants miss the community life they remember from the Sudan. Interviewees long for their relatives and familiars and even their own cultural habits. As a woman described sorrowfully

---

[283] Payne (1998), p. 60
[284] Moro (2004), p. 426
[285] cf. Moro (2004), p. 426

> there they have their traditional dances using drums, compared to this one, where people play the radio and they dance. (50, female, Equatoria)

Okello-Oloya for example explains in his work about Acholi customs that their traditions are inextricably tied to dances, music, wars, religion, domestic needs and politics.[286] These traditions and interrelations might be difficult to maintain in exile, where the practicing community is not together and exertion is limited. The Dinka for example identify themselves both socially and politically with their cattle, the absence of which has been pointed out above.[287] Certainly, in the Southern Sudan the impact of traditions also ceases in the course of land pressure, urbanization and modernization. Yet, settlement refugees have to adjust to a completely new life and sometimes lifestyle. Therefore, several participants articulated forms of homesickness, such as:

> Well, what to do when being a refugee? You have to stay under conditions like that. You cannot say that is bad. Refugee life of course, if you are in somebody's country, of course you feel homesick. You will not be like when you are in your own country. But you have to accept and learn how to live with the problem. (40, female, Equatoria)

Tension does not only occur between and within ethnic groups, but even within the smallest unit of a family. Pastoralists for example need to adapt to husbands and wives actually staying together. This includes changes in gender roles and responsibilities entailed, formerly determined by the pastoralist culture.[288]

Refugees' evaluations of integration in exile again need to be viewed in comparison to the expected situation in Southern Sudan. The issue of integration has a strong impact on movement decisions, which is underpinned by participants having been identified who against all odds – evaluating life at the settlement as decent, preferring children to continue with school in Uganda, having concerns about security in the Sudan - plan to repatriate immediately. In these cases, home comfort and the desire for reunification with relatives have been identified as decisive factors despite of all apprehensions. As Coles sug-

---

[286] cf. Okello-Oloya (1972), p. 36 ff.
[287] cf. Ismail (2005), p. 41 ff.
[288] cf. Dyson-Hudson and Dyson-Hudson (1980), p. 20 ff. also Payne (1998), p. 10 ff.

gests, "the human need to belong is more than one for protection or for the means of individual development: it is also a need to be among one's own."[289] Many have the desire to return to the place, where relatives are buried and also to be buried at home themselves. This is particularly true for elders, who fear to die in exile, without having been back to their mother country. Accordingly, the larger part of participants do not expect any problems with their reintegration into the local community. They long for their compatriots and thus assume that they are missed alike. As it was nothing but war which separated them, they expect to be welcomed warmly. Going with assistance from UNHCR, is expected to prevent them from burdening anybody. They also feel that most people have at least some relative who also left the country and therefore expect sympathy for their decisions. Some feel that they will be poor and disadvantaged when they return and therefore people will look at them with pity, but not condemn or offend them. A woman explained:

> For those people who are behind, they will not have bad hearts on us (...). This people who will be going from here to Sudan, they will be now the poorest, because for these people right now, they have things, there are even people who have opened these big big shops and others even have opened up their plantations, they are operating. Now for us, who are still here, we will be now very miserable, because we don't have these things. Those people, sometimes they may laugh at us. (69, female, Equatoria)

Reintegration on a basic social sphere is therefore expected to be uncomplicated, which goes along with the strong desire for reunification with the own kin felt by most interviewees. Expectations on reintegration strongly relate to economic factors. Refugees, who do not expect serious problems with their integration, look at themselves rather as the ones who are disadvantaged in the individual economic development and therefore do not consider themselves as competitors to remainees. Their individual educational level is throughout low, meaning they are either illiterate without any education at all or stopped at primary level. Others, however, anticipate that there will be a serious gap between the local community and themselves. Those who remained might feel that they have abandoned them in times of

289 Coles (1985) quoted in Warner (1994), p. 163

struggle and are now delaying to participate in the rehabilitation of the South, not acknowledging the official procedure of repatriation. A woman already reported the occurrence of serious conflicts between returnees and remainees in the competition for jobs, prompting the death of a refugee. Other than their compatriots in the Sudan, particularly younger refugees have gained access to education and vocational training, a clear advantage of official settlement. An interviewee anticipates:

> The way they will receive us it will not be so bad, it will not be also so good, because people they have a different mind and a different heart. Others will also receive us in a good way, other will also be jealous to us, because we came and some of our children they have got access of education like others they have completed A-Level or O-Level and others also reached to university, those who have better chances, they have reached to the university. And there, with those who have remained in Sudan, I think they didn't get any education and when we shall be going, they will think that we are going to take all the jobs, which will be in Sudan, because our children they have got education. So others will look at us in a bad manner. (33, male, Upper Nile)

Those interviewees who view themselves as economically advantaged, are more likely to expect complications with their reintegration into the local community. They are all advanced in their education, meaning they either attended secondary school or even upper school education and know how to speak English.

2.4 The infrastructure

Participants complain about their exposure to a poor infrastructural network inside the settlement and fail to balance official shortcomings. Many of them have to cover long distances to reach a health centre. Moreover, a woman reported that two of her children died in Rhino Camp Settlement, because they were not transferred to a hospital and that another woman who was refused treatment at the health unit died on her way back home. As a consequence of poverty, participants face problems on how to afford medication when it is not available for free at the centre. Again they feel the effects of the Self-Reliance Strategy. Participants recalled that the staying "was ok, they started well, but nowadays, it is now ending badly." Further discontent emerges from a shortage of boreholes and long periods of reparation in case they have broken down.

In spite of that, most participants also anticipate problems in the Sudan. The general opinion is that the war has left the infrastructure of Southern Sudan broadly underdeveloped. To tackle related problems, they are hoping for international assistance. However, scepticism due to repatriation experiences after the first civil war remains. (cf. ch. III 2.3) Others indicated that it will be themselves who have to develop the place and that educated returnees will make their contribution. They feel that others can assist, when realizing that they do not have the power to succeed themselves. When being asked about government assistance participants are more indecisive. Although many hope for assistance from the government, because "they have destroyed the South in many ways", they doubt that the government is actually willing to atone for that. Others leave it up to UNHCR, whether the government has to assist or not and show confidence that the government will obey to that. Furthermore, participants suggested that the benefits of oil and other resources will be used to develop the South. Yet, again, doubts due to former experiences shine through. The expected underdevelopment of Southern Sudan, however, does not prevent participants from repatriating, since they lack the means to access facilities inside the settlement.

2.4.1 Provision and quality of education

Education has been identified as a main stimulus, however with no distinct direction. Education is pushing participants significantly to repatriate, while at the same time holding others back. A high sensitivity for education has been recognized and participants are attributing great importance to the education of their children, or even themselves. They believe that educating their children is essential for the development and the political empowerment of the South. At the same time they intend to improve their own personal standards, particularly regarding provision for old age. All participants want to provide good education to their children, an all too often impossible task considering the aforementioned widespread poverty in the settlement. While primary school education constitutes a minor problem, secondary education defeats about half of them. The rest is either benefiting from sponsorships, does not have children of the according age, or deploys own strategies. A common one is to let children learn consecutively. While one is studying, the others try to generate an income. As soon as the first one is through, he can start contributing for the follower. It is commonly agreed upon that education in Uganda is advanced. Consequently, participants did not complain about the education itself.

> That in fact, the education here is good and the problem is just getting money, paying them is very difficult compared to the education right now there in Sudan. The country is still like that, they have not yet improved the education. (36, male, Equatoria)

Participants strongly feel a change in UNHCR policy and do not succeed in compensating the lack of sponsorships themselves.

Education in the Sudan brings about converse conflicts. While participants anticipate an improvement, simply because they will be able to generate an income and pay the fees, as seen above, they worry about the standards. The ambivalence is underpinned by the fact that of those who indicated that they are not expecting any problems with education in the Sudan, most still hope for international assistance in the improvement of schools. Two participants are even held back from repatriating because of education. Both of them are highly educated themselves and have an employment. Thus, they can afford school fees and wish their children to finish in Uganda. The questionnaire survey also revealed that there is a considerable group of youths who are learning in Uganda and intend to remain until they have finished.

2.5 Security conditions

Participants articulated concerns on how the security situation in Rhino Camp Settlement will change, once refugees have turned into the minority, leading to the desire for group movement. Same as in respect to their integration, participants again describe tensions with nationals and there is a fear of mistreatment. Former incidents, when refugees who remained behind were killed have been mentioned. The general security situation in Northern Uganda has been described in detail before. (cf. ch. III 2.4.1) Corresponding, six participants have been displaced through rebel activities in other settlements within Uganda. One participant reported how natives in Adjumani killed refugees and threw their babies into the river, also leading to displacement. An additional four participants have been displaced within Rhino Camp Settlement itself. Therefore, it can be assumed that there is a general desire among refugees for a place of more security. However, opinions on whether the Sudan can provide safety differ. A negative consequence of security threats in Southern Sudan is the resulting denial of land, which reaches across factors by fuelling the already conflicted process of land distribution and hampering agricultural growth and economic recovery.[290]

All participants from Acholiland in Equatoria agree that it is not possible to return to their home region at the moment, due to persisting intimidations by the Ugandan LRA. Acholiland is cut by the border and in the Sudan refers to the area around Torit, eastern Equatoria, where the locally called "Tong Tong" still torment people.[291] Affected participants address these problems in different ways. Some expect UNHCR to provide them with land in a peaceful area in the Sudan, others hope for the government to do so. All share the understanding that it is not possible to return to their home area, yet they do not wish to remain inside the settlement. They hope that the government will solve the problem soon. In contrast, among the questionnaire respondents a group of refugees was identified who are determined to remain in Uganda until the region is secured.
More common, and geographically less restricted, is the fear of landmines. As de-mining is considered a slow process, participants are not held back from repatriating by this, in spite of being aware of the security threat. As one participant stated:

[290] cf. Davies (1997), p. 239 ff.
[291] In September 2005, the LRA increased its activities. They crossed the Nile and also moved into western Equatoria, where they additionally strongly target the local communities since. cf. Gordon, Vandewint et al. (2007), p. 19 ff.

> Everywhere the mines are there. Even in the field they are there. Because it is not only that the mines are on the road, even in the villages they are there, for that is were the battle line was. So it is difficult to know where exactly they are placed, but even by hard luck you can find it in your field, in your village and on the road. (...) I cannot tell exactly, how I will know that the mines are cleared off, because now what I am hearing, they have started demining. But they will not demine that all, there are some which are deep in the villages, in the field, which they cannot even easily get. (...) But I am ready to go, though they have not removed them all. (male, 42, Equatoria)

The consequences of threat through mines should not be underestimated, though. Most of the victims of mines are small farmers, pastoralists, and village children. Even when people are not physically harmed, the underlying pressure still demands a high psychological prize. Widespread land denial can lead to mass impoverishment and increased morbidity.[292]

A Dinka from Bentiu is held back from returning to his home region because of oil exploitation and related intimidations. Bentiu lies within the Unity Block, one of the oldest producing oilfields in the Southern Sudan. Displacement has been escalating in that region since 1999.[293] He described:

> They [the Arabs] have chased away our people in that place and they have burned all the houses and they said that place is for the government and they call it to be a part of the Northern Sudan, which will later also cause a conflict. Like I told you, I don't want to go there because of that. There we are neighbours to the Arabs and Nuba and those Arabs they wanted now to be a part of us, to get access of petrol, because there is petrol there. If there was no petrol, they wouldn't say, they are the part of that thing. (33, male, Dinka)

Instead, this participant hopes to be provided a temporary ground to settle on in a secure part of Southern Sudan, since he does not intent to prolong his stay in exile. Apparently, violent conflicts fuel the issue of landdistribution described above. Another participant has not repatriated yet, even though he intends to return to Khartoum, which has

---

[292] cf. Kumar (1997), p. 26 ff.
[293] cf. Human Rights Watch (2003), p. 2 ff. / 247 ff.

been officially possible for some time. He is afraid of intrusions in Khartoum and fears that as someone who has left the city, he will be suspected a rebel. He described the disappearance and murder of Southern civilians in Khartoum. Indeed, during his time in Khartoum Nimeiri introduced the heavy handed approach called the kasha against Southerners, including arrests and deports, rapes, lootings, deaths and confiscated documents.[294]

2.6 Review

Repatriation is a burning issue among the refugee population. Economic, infrastructural, social and security factors have been identified to be taken into consideration by participants in their decision-making process. All factors are strongly interrelated. The desire to escape poverty and to bring about an improvement in the Sudan proved itself to have the most decisive impact. The confidence that improvement is possible is founded in the common remembrance of a good and wealthy stay in the Sudan. Even the common understanding that Southern Sudan is broadly underdeveloped does not prevent participants from planning to repatriate immediately, since they also feel discontent with the infrastructure inside the settlement and, on account of poverty, often cannot access services. Same applies for education. Consequently, participants feel that being in their home country alone will increase their possibilities and also that their future stay cannot become worse than the current one.

> Going back is at least better than that one. Even if we suffer there the same as here, we go and suffer at least in Sudan. (53, female, Equatoria)

Not to discredit Rhino Camp Settlement it shall be mentioned here that those refugees, who have self-settled before in Uganda and those who had at first sought refuge in Congo or Kenya, all agree that life in this settlement is better and that nationals even urged them to enter a settlement. Additionally, the acting agencies find themselves confronted with growing donor fatigue. Furthermore, as previously pointed out in detail, refugees have a certain role to fulfill, which requires them to appear helpless and vulnerable in order to sustain the

[294] cf. Bascom (1993), p. 40 also cf. Harir (1994), p. 16

aid situation. (cf. ch. III 1.5 and ch. IV 4.1.1) Thus, participants might tend to exaggerate their descriptions, particularly towards an international researcher. However, at the very time when interviews were conducted, a survey was carried out, which resulted in the recommendation to increase food rations. The poor fertility of the soil allocated to refugees has also been pointed out before. The understanding developed that those refugees, who exclusively rely on agriculture are the ones suffering the most, while those who have some way of generating an income are feeling a bit more satisfied and rather have the desire to prolong their stay.

The desire to genuinely integrate into a community and to reunite with the own family also strongly influences the decision making process. Most refugees are not satisfied with their integration and the community life inside the settlement. As a result they long for their homeland and all its implications. Harrell-Bond identified alcohol dependence and suicide among other factors as phenomena occurring in refugee populations without real community life;[295] occurrences were witnessed during the stay inside Rhino Camp Settlement. In the Sudan, alternatively, most participants expect easy reintegration. Others worry, that the competition for resources will seriously disrupt community life and fear ethnic disparities, a condition which will be taken up again in the following explanations on political assessment, particularly in respect to evaluations on the lasting of peace.

In respect to the issue of security, some participants fear to remain at the settlement, while others fear to return. Estimations on security in the Sudan are geographically diverse. However, apart from certain trouble spots, for the moment the area is considered secure with regard to fighting. Concerns about landmines exist, but do not influence movement decisions, primarily because no short-term solutions are available. Most participants trust that UNHCR will assess the security situation before taking them back. Thus, official repatriation itself is turned into a proof of security.

[295] cf. Harrell-Bond (2004), p. 28

3. Political assessment

There is a strong political element inherent in refugee movement. Refugees flee from their homeland because the basic bond between citizen and government has been broken. Due to this, fear has replaced trust and the own government is persecuting or rejecting some of its own.[296] In the case of the Southern Sudanese this has become true twofold. While having always been rejected and persecuted from the centre, those who fought for their liberation turned against them alike, when discipline among the rebels seriously decreased. The CPA has been concluded, but signatures alone are not enough to erase memories and deep distrust of generations. The following paragraphs capture the extent of general political involvement of refugees and perceptions of former intimidators. Furthermore, the assessment on current peace and its durability is considered and examined towards its influence on movement intentions. To embrace the entire meaning, peace will be distinguished in North-South and inner-South expectations. In accordance with the referendum, attitudes on the possibility of an independent South and its consequences will be examined. To embrace current events, John Garang's death and its effects on refugees' opinions will be captured. Again, factors are interrelated, also with the ones referred to as livelihood in this paper.

3.1 Political involvement

A general tendency for participants to be apolitical has been identified. They feel that as "someone who is not educated" they cannot assess the political future of the country and leave it to the politicians. As one participant commented on Garang:

> He is the leader, he knows what is good and what is bad (…) for them they are just following him, because he is more educated than them, whatever he is saying, it is there. (36, female, Equatoria)

Others feel that the political future lies "in God's hands". The fact that most interviewees have not entered the Sudan themselves for a long period of time, contributes to their hesitation to take a stand on the political situation. They feel that they do not really know, what is cur-

[296] cf. Stein (1986), p. 269

rently taking place in their home country. Adjustment to changes in the political system requires time. Simultaneously, as pointed out above, large numbers of civilians already lacked identification with the war itself and attributed it to the educated elite. (cf. ch. II 4.2.3) Therefore, it seems a logic consequence that they feel rather excluded from the actual occurrences and do not experience a feeling of power to intervene. A second aspect of the refugees' phlegmatic attitude on politics is the refugee status with its aforementioned implications. Official settlement tends to produce a strongly dependent population. For many becoming a refugee is synonymous with giving up their self-esteem and self-confidence, thus increasing their dependency on others.[297] Breaking out of the dependency-syndrome and re-establishing the ability to make their own decisions, might change attitudes on the extend of the own political influence. The research unit being constituted of refugees above the common school age does not allow drawing conclusions on those refugees, who have decisively advanced with education in Uganda and the impact on their political aspirations. However, as seen above, education is closely related to political exertion of influence and interviewees also consider education an important factor for the economic and political development of the South. Some interviewees indicated that they expect educated returnees, such as their own children, to get involved in politics after their return. Although not always possible, compared to conditions in the Sudan, access to education has been much easier in exile. Therefore, it remains to be seen, if educated returnees will rather refrain from politics or on the contrary form a new elite in the political arena of the Sudan.

3.2 War related intimidations

When being asked about life within the war, interviewees referred to intimidations through Northern forces as well as through Southern forces and the Ugandan LRA. In spite of the complex configuration of combating groups, they tended to generalise by only distinguishing between the "Arabs" and the "SPLAs". These terms can include the aforementioned multiplicity of contestants. The "Arabs" basically refers to government soldiers and Arab militias, and thus the central government. As pointed out ahead, the central government armed Arab tribal groups in the Northern parts of the South and thus

[297] Rogge (1994), p. 34 ff.

unleashed them against their neighbours. (cf. ch. II 4.4.1) The term "SPLAs" can include various types of SPLA factions, actual ones and defected ones, for, as it has been pointed out ahead, both main factions of the SPLA produced several splinter groups. (cf. ch. II 4.2.3) Without intending to fuel the polarization of the country into Arabs and Africans, the terminology is maintained when referring to refugees' descriptions, as they have chosen these terms themselves.

Most participants from Equatoria Province described how rebels accused them of supporting soldiers, while soldiers at the same time accused them of being rebels. They were actually "kicked like a ball between them". These denouncements are not only known between Arabs and rebels, but also within the Southern forces and even led to violent cleansings. Serving as an example, the defected commander Kerubino Kuanyin armed by the central government started raiding Bar al-Ghazal in 1994. He killed anybody, who he suspected to be supportive to Garang. Then, when Garang finally brought the area back under his control, he started killing the rest, as they *naturally* had to be supportive to Kuanyin.[298] Self-explanatory, participants describe how during these times it was not possible to trust anybody at all. Participants reported attacks on their villages including murder, rape, abduction, looting, bombings, and other intrusions. The interviewees from Upper Nile and Bahr al-Ghazal basically referred to intimidations by Arab soldiers and Arab militias. An interviewee from Wau explained that the government armed militias from Kordofan, who attacked and looted the villages in Bahr al-Ghazal.

> And there came those Arabs who also used to attack the villagers, either you are a SPLA or a civilian, they can come at daytime or nighttime and attack the area. Maybe they can come about 300 maybe 500 on horses and one horse is carrying three soldiers. (...) Then we hear the voices of clash, ta ta ta, ta ta ta, when we came out, we find them already there surrounding the area and we are in the middle. I run alone, everyone has a horse which is fallow you, and the one which was follow me, he tried to shoot me twice. Taah, taah, when he saw all the bullets had missed, he stopped and I ran into another direction, entering the bush. When I came back, I found my uncle, my brothers, some women, they are all dead, even these children.

[298] cf. Iten (1995), p. 88

As the interviewee further indicated, a major problem in Upper Nile and Bar al-Ghazal were famines:

> There was a famine, which was over Bar al-Ghazal, many people died, especially in our village. Many people died and we survived eating these leafs. (40, male, Bar al-Ghazal)

The impact of famine as a weapon of war has been described before. (cf. ch. II 4.1) The government clearly displayed its intentions, when it staged a mass deportation of refugees from camps in the outskirts of Khartoum to Wau in 1995. Even before the arrival of refugees, the government held area experienced severe famine. After having delivered the refugees, a total ban on food aid was placed, thus leading to the starvation of thousands.[299] The government and SPLA alike used military tactics that had the foreseeable consequences of creating famine, including the systematic denial of food relief.

Another interviewee from Upper Nile was abducted by the SPLA when he was only 13 years old. After his father and uncles had been killed, he was forcefully recruited and trained in Ethiopia. He then fought with the SPLA for several years and just about survived war imprisonment.

Due to these threats, most participants fled into the bush, which prompted serious, sometimes life-threatening consequences. Interviewees faced problems with nutrition, water supply, education, and satisfying any other kind of basic need. A woman reported

> that during that period in fact, we were just staying sometimes in the bush and sometimes you dig a very big hole, all of you will have to enter there, then you cook there. Now for some days, if maybe there is nobody yet, you come out for some minutes, you also go back into that hole, until even when our skin got removed completely. But we are just staying there in that what, in that hole. Sometimes if you are tired maybe you go to the bush, we are just moving around there. (...) Water is also a problem that time, even maybe the cooking, sometimes half way cooked food, then you eat. (34, female, Equatoria)

[299] cf. Spaulding and Beswick (2000), p. XVIII

A crucial factor to survive starvation without food relief is freedom of movement. However, during times of war, when famine becomes a combat strategy, this pivotal ability becomes impracticable.[300]

> That time we didn't have a rest in fact. The SPLAs could overdisturb us, they even sometimes do things like killing, now grabbing people's things. And hunger was also disturbing us that time so much, due to the pressure the SPLAs were giving us. Because from morning you have to stay in the bush, so no time for cultivating or even cooking. And because of that, in fact there was no good staying at that time. (30, female, Equatoria)

In most cases, respondents remained in the bush until rebels started penetrating them there as well. Being asked why they did not leave earlier, the predominant explanation was that they had not expected the war to last that long. Their departure to exile was further delayed by rebels' as well as soldiers' attempts to thwart the movement through road blockades. Another factor was their vulnerability on the way, as they were easy targets for both sides. Therefore they moved "from corner to corner, from bush to bush". The movement was dangerous and slow, and particularly strenuous for children.

> That in fact the movement was very difficult, because we were travelling on foot and that time, any time you are just ready to die. Like even we are going like this, sometimes they would shoot the one before and they would just drop dead and we walk by. Letting the dead body there. (34, female, Equatoria)

Leaving the Sudan, in most cases meant leaving behind all properties, as returning to the villages to pick them up was considered too dangerous. Furthermore, respondents had to cover long distances and thus could not burden themselves with luggage, which also would have revealed their intentions. Even if they managed to carry some properties they were most likely robbed on their way or at the border.

---

[300] Human Rights Watch (1990), p. 103 ff.

3.3 Attitudes towards the "Arabs"

Although most interviewees agree that Northerners and Southerners intimidated them alike, they refer to the Arabs as the origin of the war.

> What brought the war, it was just the injustice which was made by the Arabs. (36, female, Upper Nile)

There is a common understanding that the Arabs started with the oppression and the SPLA only responded to it. The oppression articulated includes the denial of education, the forced use of Arabic, the discrimination of non-Muslims, the exploitation of resources, the denial of development. Interviewees feel that the Arabs came to the Sudan for economic purposes and were accepted as traders. However, they felt superior and tried to annex the land. Participants feel that the "Sudan is for the Southerners, it is not for the Arabs". A common complaint articulated is Arabs considering themselves as "first class citizens of the country". The Northerners are clearly held responsible for having initiated the war. As Collins has pointed out, particularly the memory of the slave trade "is passed on and lingers to emerge as proof of Arab duplicity, arrogance, and contempt for the African to feed more contemporary issues of African dissatisfaction."[301] Accordingly, the majority of interviewees feel a great distrust towards the central government such as:

> I cannot trust the Northern government, I cannot trust at all. They say things opposite, when they say, you think that is the thing, you are taught different. (52, male, Equatoria)

Their suspicion is founded on former experiences and agreements which have been broken. They talked of a "trick playing from the brothers in the Northern part", which is "not from today but has been seen". A more subtle indication of discontent is the commonly used term "Jallaba" as synonym for Arab. This appellation has its origin in the slave raids, as it means trader and was used to refer to Northerners who came to exploit and raid the South.[302] The term persisted and

[301] Collins (2005), p. 27
[302] cf. Spaudlin and Beswick (2000), p. XIV

has a derogatory connotation.[303] Many interviewees however indicated that they have no problems with the Arabs ever since they have abrogated fighting. A very strong desire for peace has been identified, which seems to prevent interviewees from expressing anger towards the Arabs, as they do not wish anybody to resume fighting. However, as will be emphasized below, they do not want to stay together with the Arabs in a united country, due to their untrustworthiness. They fear that staying united will eventually lead to well-known mistreatments and opression. Others openly articulate their aversion against the Arabs. This is particularly true for the Dinka, who have fought in the SPLA. They admit that their minds are preoccupied with their anger towards the Arabs, which they relate to their traumas. Indeed, they described extraordinary human losses among their own families and attempts to overcome psychological problems through integration into society, education and counselling by TPO.

3.4 Attitudes towards the "SPLAs"

Most respondents regard the Southerners taking up arms as unavoidable counter strike considering aforementioned conditions. They feel that "happiness goes along with sorrow" and that they had to suffer for their liberation.

Although not all interviewees supported the SPLA and not all identified themselves with the war, they still respect the SPLA being compelled to fight. Other than the Arabs, who killed Southerners without comprehensible motives - e.g. in Khartoum where no battlefield existed - interviewees feel that the SPLA was obliged to pillage for self-preservation.

> That one was a voluntary work, there is no money paid to them at that time, and because of hunger and too much work they began robbing peoples' things. (57, male, Equatoria)

Most respondents indicate appreciation of the SPLA's efforts and there is a general acceptance of guerrilla war being vicious. As one participant explained:

---

[303] cf. Iten (1983), p. 56

> That actually is the life of guerrilla, even in guerrilla your brother can torture you, but as they tortured us, they have mistreated us, but still they brought peace. I have no bad feeling with them, cause they have brought us from where our eyes were closed to where our eyes will be open. Actually there is victory now in Southern Sudan. So I am feeling happy with them, more happier. (47, male, Equatoria)

Almost all interviewees indicate that they have forgiven the SPLA fighters for their intimidations and that they only desire peace now.

> We should now start a new life just as it normally happens at home, like when a husband fights with the wife, they normally solve the issue, then they join together, they stay normal. (53, female, Equatoria)

The absolution towards the rebels seems to have deeper roots than the absolution towards the Arabs, which is nourished by pragmatic considerations. However, as it will be seen in the ongoing analysis, interviewees maintain sceptic about the intentions of both sides. As pointed out before, the SPLM/A has also accessed the settlement, effects of which cannot be estimated. The frequent presence of chairmen during the interviews might have had an impact on responses regarding that theme. (cf. ch. IV 4.1)

3.5 Confidence in peace between the North and South

In spite of the great distrust towards the central government, the majority of respondents expect the peace to persist. The main argument in favour of persistency of peace is war-weariness. An interviewee explained:

> The people from North, they are tired of war. Those ones from the South, they are also tired of war. So for that case all of them are tired and we are expecting this one to be the final war in Sudan. (50, male, Equatoria)

Doubts emerge from the fact that Arabs have proved themselves as being repressive and untrustworthy and have broken several agreements before. Therefore, the vast majority favours an independent South, which actually is turned into a precondition for peace. Many indicate that the interim period will be the decisive factor. However, the larger part considers the continuation of mistreatment a predictable consequence of national unity. Therefore, although respondents expect the peace to last, they only do so under the condition of an independent South and not in bond with the North. A small minority – constituted of former SPLA fighters - feel that the war has not come to a halt yet and explained that the SPLA did neither fight for unity nor for secession, but for the expulsion of all Arabs. To them the war still continues and therefore, they did not exclude the possibility to resume armed struggle. One of them hopes that the peace agreement will allow the Southerners to get more education in the use of weapons, so they can defeat the Arabs at a later stage. Another one explained that the "first step has been taken, the second and the third shall follow". He continued:

> Like when you look at a person like me, I don't have a close relative which is still alive now (...) they were killed by Arabs. Now when I go home, I don't know where I will start, now when I go and I don't have anywhere to start, my mind will refer to my guns. I have to take my gun and see who did that. (33, male, Upper Nile)

Although these attitudes are clear minority, they underpin how essential positive perspectives for ex-combatants (as well as anybody else who is willing to take up arms) and their reintegration into society are in preventing the fragile peace agreement to be jeopardized.

3.6 Confidence in peace within the South

The larger part of interviewees expect peace within the South to persist. They consider the area being abundant and reason that a general contentment among the people will prevent tensions. Those who concede the prevalence of ethnic conflicts, do not consider them a serious problem, but rather refer to them as creations of the Arabs. It has been pointed out before, that the majority of respondents have forgiven their Southern intimidators. Moreover, they talk of a natural reconciliation period, during which tensions will placate. Additionally, they argue that the nature of the Southern government, will prevent any discontent.

> The Government of Southern Sudan will give freedom to each and every tribe in Southern Sudan to have its freedom there, so what caused conflict among the tribes, were just for leadership and some other things, grab cattle, whatever, properties, things like that. But now there is going to be rule of law there and each and everyone is going to be given his freedom to rule his county or his district, they will be under their leadership, so there will be no problem. (64, male, Bahr al-Ghazal)

Others do not share the confidence in peace within the South. Many are uncertain and demand laws and reconciliation meetings to prevent conflicts. Some even consider war within the South as unavoidable. The peace is argued to be fragile for two main reasons. One is the fear of favouritism within government rankings and unequal distribution of posts, the other agitation caused by Dinka. Both factors are closely related to the own livelihood and are also interrelated, as the SPLA is commonly viewed as a Dinka movement.[304] As one woman argued:

> The people who will maybe cause another war will be the Dinka, because they do behave like the Arabs and for them it is obvious that any time, any minute, they can also cause war. (53, female, Equatoria)

Furthermore, Dinka are accused of considering themselves being "born to rule" and thus feeling superior over other ethnic groups. In order to maintain peace, interviewees require the "national cake" to be divided equally. One interviewee reasoned:

> If you favour another tribe, you don't employ them, that peace will not last. But if things are all equal, peace will last. (52, male, Equatoria)

Participants fear favouritism along ethnic lines or functions within the war. This suspicion of inequality might be founded in former experiences, as many Equatorians complained about Dinka domination after the first civil war in addition to a general anti-SPLA attitude among Equatorians.[305] As pointed out above, after the Addis Ababa Accord the competition between delayed returnees and job holders even prompted a call for the creation of a separate Equatoria region. (cf. ch.

[304] cf. Moro (2004), p. 433
[305] cf. Simone (1994), p. 55

III 2.2) In fact, particularly considering their role in the Anya Nya I, from the beginning Equatorians lacked a prominent role in the SPLA and frequently opposed the SPLM/A's claims such as the call for a unified Southern administration.[306] The interviewed Dinka (and former SPLA-fighters), however, do not claim preferential treatment for themselves. One asks for compensation for the years he spent fighting, another one does not even request that, because he feels that he "was fighting for the heart of the land and the freedom of the people". In accordance with the other Dinka he feels that

> all those positions, they are free to any person who will qualify for any post, because that war was fought to bring freedom to the Southerners. So if one of the Southerners qualifies for any post and he didn't fight, there is no problem. Even if he had been with the government or he was against the SPLA, there is nothing, provided he is a Southerner, we welcome that. (64, male, Bahr al-Ghazal)

3.7 Independence

The vast majority of interviewees favours an independent South. Actually, not a single participant articulated the wish to remain united with the North. However, several indicated that the interim period had to be used to assess the situation and that afterwards both alternatives were conceivable options. Participants again refer to the Arabs' untrustworthiness. As hinted on before, they feel that union will lead to well-known mistreatments and that it is time for the South to emancipate itself from Northern restrictions.

> That in fact the independent country is the best, because now for people in the South, they know what is good for them and what is bad. Since those people used to oppress us because of our things, now let them be alone in their fight. If they want to oppress themselves they should also do it themselves in their fight there. (36, male, Equatoria)

Interviewees do not sense a genuine interest of the North to contribute to the development of the South and feel that they have suffered long enough. Being a resource rich region, they pursue a prosperous autonomous Southern entity. Others go as far as demanding the entire Sudan for the people of the South, arguing that the Arabs have no

[306] cf. Branch and Mampilly (2005), p. 3 ff.

inherited right to the Sudan and should no longer be tolerated. A woman explained:

> This country is not for the Arabs, it is our country. Now for this people with their bad manners, they came from their country and they oppressed people from this country. And at last right now they want the country to be independent; they want to divide, which is not favourable. I am not happy about it (...) the country doesn't belong to the Arabs; it is supposed to be for the people from the South. (30, female, Equatoria)

3.8 The impact of John Garang's death

Garang's outstanding position among Southerners, who viewed him as their redeemer, has been pointed out above. (cf. ch. II 5.3) On the day of his death, he was actually expected to give a speech at Yei. Awaiting the leader, the entire town was filled with an atmosphere of high agitation. Only the following day news about his death was revealed. The researcher herself then had been back to the settlement. The atmosphere there was the very opposite. Grief and despair were in the air. Several mourning ceremonies followed. The pain of refugees about the loss of the person they had put all their trust in was omnipresent. In consequence, respondents grew reluctant to repatriate. Refugees argued that the security situation and the durability of peace between North and South might be affected. Although not all respondents went as far as considering the postponement of their repatriation, the vast majority expressed concerns on the consequences for the peace process. As one respondent put it:

> There was real guarantee for the peace to succeed when the first vice president was in control. He knows the Arabs well and could deal with them according. Now that he is dead, I don't know what will happen. (38, female, Equatoria)

In respect to the durability of peace within the South, his death was not attributed to have such a decisive impact. Very few expected negative effects on stability inside the South, such as

> the late vice president was capable of unifying all groups in the South. I doubt whether his successor will have the same ability. (56, male, Equatoria)

Others even took the manner in which Southerners have responded to Garang's death as a positive indication for stability within the South. They feel that "Southerners have shown unity, maturity and democracy".[307]

3.9 Review

Generally speaking, reluctance on giving any kind of political statement or even getting involved oneself has been recognized. Still, several estimations and their consequences could be established. Participants described how they have been exposed to great suffering during the war, which was created by Northerners and Southerners alike. While the Arabs are blamed for oppressing the South and starting the war, the SPLA is rather excused, because they defended themselves and the South, enlightened the ones who did not see the oppression and also because the cruel aspects of guerrilla war enjoy general acceptance. The strong urge for independence reinforces the conclusion that participants are not as forgiving towards the Arabs as they verbalize to be. They do not ask for revenge or retaliation, but want to leave the war behind them, develop their country and lead a pacific life. Contrary, the forgiveness towards the SPLA is underpinned by feelings of sympathy and gratitude. The majority only longs for peace, equality and proper sharing. Attitudes towards the Arabs and the SPLAs alike strongly depend on the individuals' experience and memories of life inside the Sudan. Noticeably, although many interviewees expressed doubts on the peace between North and South, no one is certain about the war resuming. The main argument is war-weariness. But, within the South alone, voices even claim that there is definitely going to be war, for which blame is basically put on favouritism and Dinkas' disdainful behaviour. These worries have, in parts, been strengthened through the unexpected death of Garang. Still, suspicion emerged if talks of forgiveness for Southern intimidators are more of a narrative, maybe even influenced by the SPLM/A themselves, than actual opinions. (cf. IV 4.1) The throughout occur-

[307] Information on Garang's death exclusively derive from the questionnaire material, as no more interviews were carried out after the crucial date. Distribution took place in September 2005 when news was still fresh and consequences not conceivable, yet.

rence of mentions related to ethnicity reveal a dreadful potential of conflict concerning that issue.

4. Case Review

Since the human experience is the focus of this work, so far, it has been attempted to fill all categories with the participants' matters and concerns. Before concluding this work, five distinct cases shall be exemplary presented in detail, as to display the individual constellation every participant embraces and provide a better understanding of individual contexts. Cases have been chosen in a way that allows grasping various personal realities and priorities, which also require different kinds of assistance.

Mama Palaminia (65, female, Equatoria)

Mama Palaminia does not remember her age. She thinks she is older than 50, while the interpreter and researcher assumed she was at least 65. She feels a strong bond to her homeland and wants to return to the place where her husband and her sons are buried. When the war started to affect her region, she hid herself in the bush. However, when the son's wife died in exile, he came to collect her to watch after their baby. She had not left on her own accord, but was glad that someone was leading her out of the chaos. She emphasizes that during these days she still had the power to walk the entire way by herself. But Mama Palaminia has grown old in exile. Nowadays, she has to rely on her daughter-in-law's and her grandchildren's assistance. She lost her refugee status when she tried to spontaneously repatriate, and does neither feel well assisted nor well respected by the refugee population. She hopes to be reregistered soon, as she wants to take advantage of the official repatriation immediately. She has very nostalgic memories and is scared that she might die before official repatriation starts. When speaking of incidences that might delay her repatriation she gets furious. She asks herself: "Am I not going back to Sudan to see the rivers, the hills that are there in my land?" She is desperate to go home, to "the place where she planted some mangos" and "where there is love". Her son is supposed to guide her and to prepare the place. She expects to be welcomed warmly and does not see any reasons at all why refugees should remain in exile. She has seen that there are churches and hospitals in the Sudan and that people started settling and leading a happy life. Interestingly, as she has been to the Sudan recently, her narrations are not lacking foundation. However, she is dazzled by her boundless homesickness and does not consider any shortcomings, such as the poor infrastructure. She even experienced some hostilities when she went back and a relatives' wife was the one preventing her from settling. Yet, she is expecting an improvement in the Sudan in any respect. In accordance with her religion, she has forgiven all intimidators. Mama Palaminia is fighting against the time, as she wants to close her life in the Sudan. Thus, she is not considering long-term development, but only current conditions.

Esta (51, female, Equatoria)

Esta is a 51 years old widow and has, due to the early deaths of her parents, not received any formal education. Yet, in the Sudan she was able to grow and sell foodstuffs. She did not want to leave the Sudan and was hoping that the Arabs would not enter into the countryside. After they started penetrating them there after all, she saw no any other chance but seeking exile in Uganda. In her view, the war was a war about resources, which she traces back to "the Arabs who want their place where there are minerals." Once official repatriation has started, she wants to leave Rhino Camp immediately. That is above all because of food shortage and lack of education for her children. As she explained

> nowadays even this UNHCR they have some containers, just this size, for giving the maize and they will tell you that you eat this one for one month, which will not even reach a month, it will not even reach a week.

She has faith into the fertility of the soil in the Sudan and believes that there she will be able to grow enough to start selling goods again, with the money of which, she plans to provide education for her children. She believes that it will take some two years, before she has acquired enough for the first child to start. Because her properties in the Sudan have all been burned, and because UNHCR has also accommodated them in exile, she expects help for the transitional period, before she reaches self-sufficiency. She expects to be received well by the local community and has confidence into the new system in the Sudan, because Garang "has left the jungle and is now in the office." Yet, she is not certain about whether peace will remain with the North and neither within the South. All this lies in the hands of the "big, big people". She certainly favours an independent South, as the Arabs have disturbed them for so long that she is sure they will continue with the very behaviour. Therefore, there is no any other alternative than secession. She is unsatisfied with life in Uganda and sure that after a transitional period of adjustment and hardship, she will be able to lead a content life in the Sudan and most importantly provide the education that has been denied to herself for her children.

Martin (41, male, Equatoria)

Martin is 41 years old and highly educated. He was born to a prosperous man, whose business collapsed during the Anya Nya war. He received his education partly in the Sudan and partly in exile in Uganda. After the first civil war, he started working for GTZ and travelled to various African and western countries. When Yei was attacked, he joined a neighbour in his vehicle together with his family and left for Uganda. He does not share the same horrific memories of most of his compatriots in exile. When Martin arrived in Uganda, he started to work for the former implementing partner of UNHCR immediately. Thus, in comparison to others, he faced fewer problems with establishing himself in exile. Ever since his department was handed over to the district in the course of the Self-Reliance Strategy, he has been unemployed. However, his wife is working for TPO and still generating an income. Unless speaking of education, he refers to problems at the settlement in the third person. Four dependents came to join him in exile, and so far he his providing education for all of them, plus his own two children. However, he will not be able to continue like that for long. Martin wants to return to the Sudan as soon as possible. He does not cultivate himself and thus is left without a task. Although his wife's income allows him a relatively decent life, he is not satisfied. He feels as if his life was put on halt and tries to find self-realization in drawing pictures. Martin also desires to reunite with his family and has already travelled to the Southern Sudan on a frequent basis. He is tired of the dependency at the settlement and longs for his home, which he wants to develop. Furthermore, he seeks for self-fulfillment and personal development, as well as economic improvement.

Emanuel (52, male, Equatoria)

Emanuel is 52 years old and working as a teacher. He remembers the Sudan as the place, where he was oppressed by the Arabs and humiliated by the SPLA. It is not his first time to exile and he does not want to return, yet. Emanuel considers the war necessary and good, as the Southerners had to liberate themselves. However, for himself he found it more important to flee and take his children to a place where they can receive education.

Education is also the reason why he wants to remain in Uganda. He feels comfortable and safe in exile and expects severe competition and violence between educated returnees and the uneducated society. He calls for a fair and equal sharing of the national cake, in order to prevent another war. Otherwise he considers the area secure, but still wants to monitor the development. Only when his children are well prepared he is ready to repatriate. He does not intend to remain in Uganda for good, as he cannot afford university education there and aspires to high-ranking posts for his children, which they will only be able to receive in their homeland. He does not express any emotional bond to his homeland, which he is holding in bad memories. He is driven by economic factors and wants to maximize opportunities for his children, so that they can provide a comfortable life for him in his old age.

Luka (33, Dinka, Upper Nile)

Luka has a completely different biography than the majority of refugees in Rhino Camp Settlement, which leads to different attitudes and demands. He is 33 years old and comes from Upper Nile. When the war, which he describes as a liberation-war, reached his home region, he fled with his father and uncle to stay with the Nuba. There, he was eventually captured by the SPLA at the age of 13 and his father and uncle killed by the rebels. After he had received military training in Ethiopia, he started to fight for the SPLA in the Sudan, up to when he was captured and taken into war prison. He escaped just about before starving to death and developed serious mental disorders. After his escape he was promised mental counselling by a SPLA commander, but instead requested to take up arms again. He fled once again and after a short time in Kenya and various different stations in Uganda, he finally settled down in Rhino Camp Settlement, where he lives now with his wife and five children. In Uganda Luka received counselling from TPO, which helped him to stabilise his psychological condition. He also received his first formal education, which helped him to calm down. Yet, he had to drop out prematurely due to financial shortcomings. He faces serious problems in sustaining himself and his family, since he has not been trained to cultivate. Because of the poor and insecure staying inside the settlement, Luka wants to repatriate as soon as possible. Coming from the oil-rich region of Bentiu where violent conflict is still prevalent he hopes for civil support and temporary provision of land from sympathizers, until he can return to his home region. He is also in hope for assistance in re-establishing livelihood in the Sudan, as returnees “shall be new people in that land, because [they] have overstayed away”. Above all he desires free education for himself and his children and financial compensation for those years that he fought for the SPLA. In general, he feels that people have to be compensated for their contributions during the war, such as civilians who did not fight themselves, but yet provided food and accommodation to the rebels. He suspects the war between North and South to resume in some 3-5 years, as the GoS cannot be trusted. At the same time he expressed willingness to take up arms again himself, if implementations and compensations are denied. He has very hard, maybe irreconcilable, feelings towards the Arabs, who according to him feel superior.

> Though they look brown [the Arabs] and we look black, we have the same blood and we have the same mind, what Arab can do, I can also do. If we access the same education, I will do it even better than an Arab. So let them consider us like people in the same country. We don't want Arabs to be in Sudan. So if it is not possible to chase them out now, little by little we shall also do our level best to get rid of them. We have one objective, to get independent. That will be only one step and we shall plan for a second step and then the final one will come and it is ok.

According to him, the Southerners have not fought for Garang being vice-president but president of the entire Sudan, thus the war has not been concluded, yet.

VI Conclusions

1. Movement decisions and future expectations

The prime intention of the presented work is to capture the context of how refugees cope with the fact that the peace agreement has been signed and repatriation is materializing into an official option including refugees' anticipations of the new area of peace in the Sudan.

Typically, the refugee experience is divided into four phases: pre-flight, flight, temporary settlement, and resettlement or repatriation.[308] For the research population options how to close the cycle are limited, as no form of resettlement is truly offered. Thus, repatriation is the only possible solution and movement decisions are limited to the moment of when to move. While repatriation is the end of the Refugee Cycle, it is also the beginning of a new cycle of social, political and economic reintegration, and regional development. Only when having successfully established oneself again, the gross experience comes close to an end. Expectations on the Return Cycle are crucial for movement decisions.

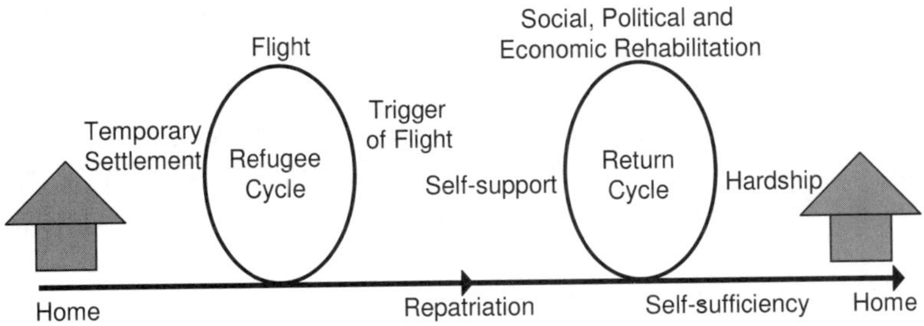

Figure 3: The gross refugee experience

[308] cf. Ager (1999), p. 3

The refugee cycle has been opened with the active devastation of the Southern Sudan from the North and from within the South itself. The persistence of war resulted in participants being in exile between six and eighteen years. The transference from the Sudan to the Rhino Camp Settlement was not as simple as the figure suggests, as most participants hid in the bush for several months or years, and a considerable number came via Congo or Kenya. They had to undergo harsh conditions on the flight and to a great extent experienced insecurities and displacement even in exile. By crossing the border, citizens have become refugees, who are by definition persons, who "owing to a well-founded fear"[309] were compelled to leave their country. Official recognition as a refugee is an ambivalent condition. While registration enables, it also restricts and refugees have to give up great extents of their self-determination in order to receive assistance. Ugandan policy stipulates that all refugees and asylum seekers must live in designated areas.[310] Yet, frequently, neither the government nor the agencies compensate accordingly for movement denials and other constraints, such as restrictions on the issuing of working permits.[311] Sometimes, neither political nor socio-economic needs of refugees are fully met, who live in insecure areas and are exposed to poverty. Refugees are denied the right to cross into their homeland and thus to start creating a new livelihood. In addition, they can not repatriate when they wish, but have to wait for the official start. This might not only lead to a disadvantage in re-establishing themselves, but also created a fear of hostile reception inside the South among refugees, as others have already started to develop the country. Too often, refugees are referred to as "masses of desperate people in need of assistance"[312] and thus denied their individual background and aspirations.

The signature of the Comprehensive Peace Agreement between the Government of the Sudan and the SPLM/A changed those circumstances, which have been crucial for the recognition as refugee. However, peace alone does not facilitate the refugees' safe return and well-being in the Sudan. Refugees found their movement decisions

[309] UNHCR (1997), p. 51
[310] cf. Bagenda and Hovil (2003), p. 14, also Stein (1986), p. 275 ff.
[311] cf. Payne (1998), p. 125
[312] Moro (2004), p. 426

similar as migrants on a balance between personal aspirations and information available on wider structural conditions, which they evaluate. Return migrants may not attain full knowledge of the range of opportunities at home and choose accordingly to a limited subset of possible alternatives.[313] Although home countries, host countries, the international community and political fronts in exile might have an interest in maintaining or receiving refugee influxes, misinforming refugees contradicts with the voluntariness of their movement. The type of signals the host government sends out to the refugees will greatly influence their desire to return home.[314] Thus, it is important to note, that the SPLM/A has an interest in the refugees returning as soon as possible.[315] Kosers' "model of a refugee information system" portrays the information flows. Accordingly, the conditions at home generate information, which are transferred through agents to the refugees, who will evaluate them. The components are not static, but altered through external inputs.

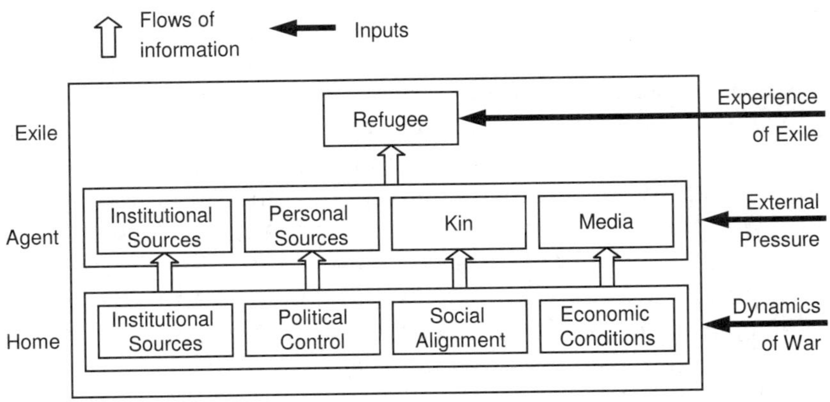

Figure 4: Model of a refugee information system[316]

[313] cf. Koser (1993), p. 173 ff.
[314] cf. Rogge (1994), p. 32 ff. also Koser (1993), p. 178
[315] Personal correspondence with Johnson Juma and Peter Otim (Yei, 29.07.2005)
[316] Koser (1993), p. 178

Refugees in close proximity to the border are clearly better informed than those at a distance from the border.[317] This definitely applies for the research population, as some participants have travelled themselves to the Sudan. Others refer to relatives or just people who move and provide information. Additionally, UNHCR is considered a main source of information. Rogge suggest that refugees often place a high degree of trust in agency workers.[318] However, the refugees still assess the reliability of information and come to their own conclusions, which will determine their movement. Not only future perspectives in the Sudan are decisive for movement intentions but also the assessment of the current staying and the future staying in Uganda. If nothing else the case review has revealed that each participant has his very own set of personal attributes and motivations. Yet, parallels have been identified and allow for categorizations.

The contentedness with life at the settlement strongly depends on the refugees' economic standards. Naturally, the worse the situation, the greater the desire for improvement. With the introduction of the Self-Reliance Strategy conditions inside the settlement have worsened; access to health-services mostly requires money and scholarships have also been reduced. Reasons vary. On the one hand, integration has stipulated the handing over to the district; on the other hand, the settlement is not considered an emergency anymore, leading to donor fatigue. Furthermore, as repatriation has become an option, ambivalence on whether to invest into exile or into the Sudan emerges. The assessment of conditions at the settlement and the expectations of the future, such as emerging security threats, are compared with expected conditions in the Sudan. These are, as has been pointed out, partly depending on the information system, partly on direct personal investigations and partly on personal attributes and preferences.

Upon return, most refugees anticipate a transitional period of extraordinary hardship, for which they are in hope of international assistance. The majority has indicated wanting to return to their home villages and start cultivation again. Only a minority desires to move into the cities, most likely for reasons of education and occupation. Rogge has displayed the stages of reintegration of rural refugees as follows:

---

[317] cf. Koser (1993), p. 178
[318] cf. Rogge (1994), p. 33

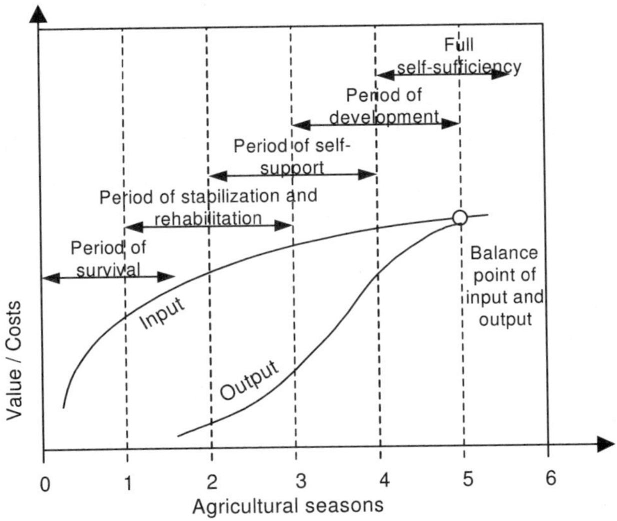

Figure 5: Stages in the process of reintegration of rural refugees[319]

As the figure suggests, there is a time-lag between the need of heavy inputs and the production of outputs that allow self-sufficiency or even profit. If that phase is prolonging, returnees might be drawn into urban areas.[320] The individual expectations of the transitional period up to self-sufficiency and the anticipated possible economic wealth play a major role in determining the movement decision. Those who see an advantage in remaining in exile, such as economic wealth or education, may decide to remain. Those who do not see any advantage, feel that they have nothing to loose and are more likely to choose the uncertainty of return. Logically, the access to institutions such as schools and hospitals is more important then the quality, if one is unable to benefit from it. It is important to note that a large number of participants are not expressing a plain natural desire of improvement of their economic and infrastructural situation. They rather refer to conditions at Rhino Camp Settlement as intolerable and inhuman. Therefore they are likely to return immediately. The distinction between this and repatriation under duress is debatable.

---

[319] Rogge (1994), p. 36
[320] Rogge (1994), p. 34 ff.

Next to economic and infrastructural factors, social ones have their influence. While participants complain about heteronomy and dependency, poor community life, fear of the nationals and restrictions of rights in Uganda, they yearn for home comfort and the reunification with their kin. They also want to return to the places where they have buried their relatives and particularly elders express a strong desire to return, as they expect better community structures to support them and also want to close their lives at home.

A further determining factor is the political situation in the Sudan, but also in Uganda. Participants indicated that they wanted to leave before presidential elections in Uganda, as they feared insurgencies. With Museveni's re-election in February 2006, a common concern among refugees has been eased, as he is considered to be supportive to refugees. The political situation in the Sudan is commonly attributed to be stable. Interestingly, participants rather fear conflicts within the South than in confrontation with the North. Both sides are estimated to be tired of fighting and to have come to the conclusion that there is no military solution. However, independence after the interim period is turned into a precondition for peace with the North, as the continuation of oppression in a united country is considered unavoidable. The majority clearly seeks for peace, while only a small group, basically consisting of Dinka, voiced that the war has to be continued.[321] This conforms with the behaviour of Dinka being perceived as a possible threat to peace. Within the South conflicts on equality and sharing are expected and sometimes result in reluctance to repatriate. Refugees worry that they will be passed over in the distribution processes to the benefits of those who have directly or indirectly participated in the war. The manner in which land distribution will be carried out, might further fuel ethnic disparities. The strong fear of favouritism and related violent conflicts has not only been identified among refugees, but also among remainees, who worry that better educated returnees might take all jobs and posts. Herewith, a high potential of conflict within the South has been identified that might endanger the peace.

[321] The special situation of the Dinkas has been pointed out. To reconcile hard feelings against their Northern intimidators is apparently more difficult than among other ethnic groups.

Garang's death decreased trust into the peace among refugees. Yet, they have a strong desire for peace and are therefore reluctant to feelings of retaliation and anger. There is a major difference between the perception of Northern and Southern groups, although they are said to have intimidated civilians alike. While refugees feel deep distrust towards the central government, they have a greater understanding for the SPLA. This is particularly important as a common condition preventing repatriation is the continuation in power of the regime that originally caused the exodus.[322] Being willing to forgive the SPLA and given the fact that the Southern Sudan is provided autonomy, a political fundament for repatriation is created.

All estimations are founded on the described information system, but also on personal attributes. Each individual has their own context of demographic data such as age, gender, educational and economic status, as well as personal attributes such as memories of the Sudan, duration of the stay in exile, experiences in exile, previous repatriations, political interest, social relations and so forth. The form of settlement is taking its impact as well. The research has revealed that there is a sense of group movement in the settlement. Bascom further identified that camp refugees, due to their general dependency, are more likely to rely on leaders to lead cooperative decisions to repatriate.[323] The following figure summarizes the context of refugees' decisions.

[322] cf. Stein (1986), p. 270
[323] cf. Bascom (1994), p. 236

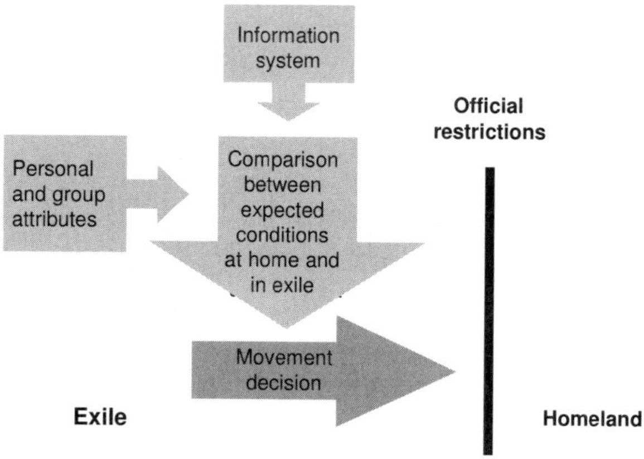

Figure 6: A return migrant's decision-making process

The information system and the process of comparison, supplemented by group attributes and a set of personal attributes, determine, whether refugees plan to repatriate or to remain in exile. The consequences yet depend on the official facilitation of the movement.

2. Evaluation of methodology

Using a triangulated qualitative research design proved to be very sufficient. The intention of the work was to explore an unfamiliar field of research. Therefore, as little pre-knowledge was available, the Grounded Theory as an explorative approach was prioritised. The dynamic combination of data collection, evaluation, selection of participants and further data collection, provided the necessary flexibility to adjust to all phenomena identified. However, when only a short research period is aspired, the Grounded Theory will not provide the expected outcomes. Indeed, a wide timeframe and an atmosphere proper to reflect are crucial to the success of the Grounded Theory. Furthermore, in Grounded Theory a single phenomenon is identified to form the core of the research and is deeply explored. This turned out to be too narrow and specific as a frame for the particular intention of this research. Thus, with the time-frame being too tight and the methodology not exactly fitting the intention of the research, elements of the Qualitative Content Analysis have been included. The researcher had to realize that in some cases her sheer presence already manipulated participants' responds. It is assumed that the entangled relationship between international aid workers and refugees influenced the relation between refugees and the researcher. In order to create a counter-balance, the interpreters were trained to stress on the academic purpose of the work, however, the desired affects failed to fully appear. This can partly be traced back to the persisting and correct assumption that outcomes have an impact beyond university level. Furthermore, the fact that the researcher had come from abroad was perceived as an indication that she might be able to assist, thus leading to the desire to appear vulnerable. However, equally problematic was the lacking anonymity in a vis-à-vis interview, particularly when it came down to issues which compete with the official refugee status. The presence of chairmen might have further influenced responds, maybe in favour of SPLM/A policy. To balance some of these insufficiencies a questionnaire was designed. This allowed the researcher to collect data, without revealing her entire identity. However, for ethic reasons, the purpose was clearly stated and anonymity unexceptionally kept. In order to maintain the qualitative and explorative character of the work, most questions were kept open. Indeed, some interesting outcomes were revealed. Refugees displayed a greater openness, even on sensitive issues. Furthermore, when including younger respondents, the research received a new outlook. As the conduction outdated the crucial date of Garang's death, even these influences could be measured. Thus, trying a questionnaire survey in this research turned out to be worthwhile.

3. Future perspectives

The fundamental precondition for repatriation, the conclusion of the Comprehensive Peace Agreement between the Government of the Sudan and the SPLM/A, has been met. The research, however, has revealed that such calculation is merely theoretic and the movement decision consists of a complex combination of factors, both relating to conditions in exile and in the homeland. It was not the intention of this work to foresee how refugees respond, when official repatriation has started, but to illuminate the context in which decisions are made. Nonetheless, a considerable part of participants indicated that for them official repatriation could not come soon enough and provided plausible reasoning. However, it remains questionable if they will actually follow through with their decision. Experience has shown that refugees often employ an image of the perfect home country to carry them through hardship in exile and when it becomes possible, they enter reflections on what actually to expect when going back. Indeed, as Warner points out, the home refugees remember will have changed during years of absence, same as they have changed themselves. Thus, refugees are repatriating to conditions unknown.[324] Furthermore, during the lengthy stay, refugees have become accustomed to the host country, as well as to the settlement structures. Refugees have to break out of the welfare syndrome acquired during many years of settlement life. The intentions to repatriate need proper facilitation. Sufficient and objective information has to be made available to refugees to guarantee well-founded decision makings and thus keep repatriation as voluntary as possible. As pointed out, refugees enter a new cycle of dependency and readjustment when returning to the Sudan. Their success is crucial to encouraging those refugees, who take a wait and see position. In fact, the entire region has to be developed, as refugees (and remainees) might have the capacity to adjust, but still fail due to a completely destroyed economic, social or physical infrastructure.[325] Kumar suggests three essential and interrelated elements of transition: Restoration, structural reform and institution building.[326] They all refer to efforts to rebuild political, economic and social structures of war-torn societies. Same as the individual undergoes a period of transition before reaching personal normalcy, the entire society does. This requires substantial and sustained economic and technical assistance. Additionally, the Sudan has the advantage of rich resources, which can be used for the development of the country. Already mentioned, the repatriation after the first civil war demonstrated serious insufficiencies, [327] which parts of the refugee population experienced themselves.

[324] cf. Warner (1994), p. 68 ff. also Kumar (1997), p. 17
[325] cf. Rogge (1994), p. 45 ff.
[326] cf. Kumar (1997), p. 2 ff.
[327] cf. Akol (1994), p. 93 f.

The successful integration of refugees has proved to be crucial to the durability of peace and vice-versa.[328] Reconciliation is an essential factor in that process. Not only political leaders, but entire communities have to find a way of peaceful coexistence (maybe alongside former enemies). A stable democracy is the political system most likely to facilitate the coexistence of differences and can be seen as a "system for managing conflict".[329] The history of the Sudan displays a great abuse of ethnic attributes, the repetition of which urgently has to be prevented, particularly in respect to the distribution of land and occupation. Reconciliation is a long-term process involving the entire community. Having received education in exile, refugees bring along intellectual potential desperately needed for the good of the entire country. Yet, only if remainees facilitate the economic progress of returnees will those be able to actually advance and to use their skills for their individual as well as the regional development. Reintegration and reconciliation are crucial factors in this process and concerns of returnees and remainees have to be considered alike. Furthermore, refugees seem to be capable, but not confident or interested enough to enter the political arena, a potential that still needs to be activated (and carefully integrated).

It has become clear that the generalisation of refugees as a homogenous group is misleading and increasing their vulnerability. To guarantee their protection, it is therefore strongly recommended to consider refugees within the repatriation and rehabilitation process in a more differentiated manner. Specific needs require individually targeted responses. If another refugee trail out of the Sudan is sought be prevented, the reintegration of all returnees, the development of the entire region and political stability have to be addressed full heartedly and their interdependence acknowledged. A general improvement in the human rights situation in the Sudan is essential and individuals as well as groupings have to reconcile. Takei explained that "people can forget what has formerly happened, if past events are not relevant to their current life; collective memory is activated when people perceive that the patterns of the past are being repeated in the present."[330] Only if the peace is maintained, the refugees' deep yearning for a

[328] cf. Johnson (1994), p. 126 ff.
[329] Bloomfield, Barnes et al (2005), p. 10
[330] Takei (1998) in Moro (2004), p. 426

decent and pacific life in their home country can be met. However the peace is fragile, particularly after Garang's death, and a solution for the South does not equal a solution for the entire country. Refugees seem to be ready to give the venture a try. It is now up to the two governments and the concerned agencies to facilitate the refugees' safe return and to create an environment that will allow them to take up a normal and peaceful life.

References

Acker, Frank van (2004): Uganda and the Lord's Resistance Army: The new order no one ordered. In: African Affairs, 103 (412), p. 335-357.

Ager, Alastair (ed.) (1999): Perspectives on the refugee experience. In: Refugees: Perspectives on the Experience of Forced Migration. GB: Biddles Ltd.

Akol, Joshua O. (1994): A crisis of expectations: Returning to Southern Sudan in the 1970s. In: Allen, T. and Morsink H. (eds.): When Refugees Go Home. Trenton: Africa World Press.

Allen, Tim and Morsink, Hubert (eds.) (1994): Introduction: When Refugees Go Home. In: When Refugees Go Home. Trenton: Africa World Press.

Ali, Taisier M. and Matthews, Robert O. (eds.) (1999): Civil War and Failed Peace Efforts in Sudan. In: Civil Wars in Africa: Roots and Resolutions. Montreal et al: McGill-Queen's University Press.

Alier, Abel (1992): Southern Sudan: Too many agreements dishonoured. London et al: Ithaca Press Reading.

Al-Rahim, Muddathir'abd (1969): Imperialism and Nationalism in the Sudan: A Study in Constitutional and Political Development 1899-1956. Oxford: Clarendon Press.

Anand, Renu M. (1993): African Refugees: An Overview. New Delhi: Khama Publishers.

Anderson, G. Norman (1999): Sudan in Crisis: The Failure of Democracy. Gainesville et al: University Press of Florida.

Arkell, Anthony J. (1961): A History of the Sudan: From the Earliest Times to 1821. Westport: Greenwood Press.

Assefa, Hizkias (1987): Mediation of Civil Wars, Approaches and Strategies: The Sudan Conflict. Boulder: Westview.

Bagenda, Emmanuel and Hovil, Lucy (2003): Sudanese Refugees in northern Uganda: From one conflict to the next. In: Forced Migration Review, 16, 14-16.

Baldo, Suliman (2005): Could peace unravel? In: Forced Migration Review, 24, 25-27.

Bakwesegah, Chris J. (1994): Forced Migration in Africa and the OAU Confention. In: Adelman, H. and Sorenson, J. (eds.): African Refugees: Development Aid and Repatriation. Boulder et al: Westview Press.

Barnett, Michael and Finnemore, Martha (2004): Rules for the World: International Organisations in Global Politics. Ithaca, London: Cornell University Press.

Bascom, Johnathan (1993): 'Internal refugees': the case of the displaced in Khartoum. In: Black, R. and Robinson, V. (eds.): Geography and Refugees: Patterns and Processes of Change. London, New York: Belhaven Press.

Bascom, Jonathan (1993)a: The Peasant Economy of Refugee Resettlement in Eastern Sudan. In: Annals of the Association of American Geographers, 83(2), 320-346.

Bascom, Johnathan (1994): The dynamics of refugee repatriation: the case of Eritreans in eastern Sudan. In: Gould, W.T.S. and Findlay, A.M. (eds.): Population Migration and the Changing World Order. Chichester: John Wiley and Sons.

Beshir, Mohamed Omer (1975): The Southern Sudan: From Conflict to Peace. USA: Harper and Row Publishers, Inc.

Bloomfield, David, Barnes, Teresa et al (eds.) (2005): Reconciliation after Violent Conflict: A Handbook. Stockholm: International IDEA.

Both, Lam Peter (2002): South Sudan: Forgotten Tragedy. Calgary: University of Calgary Printing Services.

Branch, Adam and Mapilly, Zachariah C. (2005): Winning the war, but loosing the peace? The dilemma of SPLM/A civil administration and the tasks ahead. In: Journal of Modern African Studies, 43 (1), 1-20.

Breidlid, Anders (2006): Resistance and Education: Counter-Hegemonic Struggle in Southern Sudan. In: Nordisk Pedagogik, 26 (1), 16-29.

Brody, Eugene (1994): The Mental Health and Well-Being of Refugees: Issues and Directions. In: Marsella, A. J., Bornemann, T. et al (eds.): Amidst Peril and Pain: The Mental Health and Well-Being of the World's Refugees. Washington: American Psychological Association.

Burnham, Gilbert M., Rowley, Elizabeth A. et al (2003): Quality Designs: A Planning Methodology for the Integration of Refugee and Local Health Services, West Nile, Uganda. In: Disasters, 27 (1), 54-71.

Burr, J. Millard and Collins, Robert O. (1995): Requiem for the Sudan: War, Drought, and Disaster Relief on the Nile. Boulder, San Francisco, Oxford: Westview Press.

Butt, Audrey (1964): The Nilotes of the Sudan and Uganda. London: International African Institute.

Collins, Robert O. (2005): Civil Wars and Revolution in the Sudan: Essays on the Sudan, Southern Sudan and Darfur, 1962 – 2004. Hollywood: Tsehai.

Collins, Robert O. (1999): Africans, Arabs and Islamists: From the Conference Tables to the Battlefields in the Sudan. In: African Studies Review, 42 (2), 105-123.

Collins, Robert O. (1975): The Southern Sudan in Historical Perspective. New Brunswick: Transaction Publishers.

Colville, Rupert (1994): Unsafe and Insecure. In: Refugees, II, 19-21.

Davies, Paul (1997): Mines and Unexploded Ordnance in Cambodia and Laos: Understanding the costs. In: Kumar, Krishna: Rebuilding Societies After Civil War: Critical Roles for International Assistance. Boulder, London: Lynne Rienner Publishers.

De Lorenzo, Mauro (1999): The security situation for refugees in Uganda. In: Migration world, Vol S, 23-25.

Deng, Francis M. (1984): The Dinka of the Sudan. Prospect Heights: Waveland Press.

Deng, Francis M. (1995): War of Visions: Conflict of Identities in the Sudan. Washington D.C.: The Brookings Institution.

Deng, Francis M. (2001): Country Survey: Sudan – Civil War and Genocide. In: Middle East Quarterly, 8 (1), 13-21.

Deng, Francis M. (2005): African renaissance: towards a New Sudan. In: Forced Migration Review, 24, 6-8.

Deng, Luka Biong (2005): The Comprehensive Peace Agreement: will it also be dishonoured? In: Forced Migration Review, 24, 15-16.

Diekmann, Andreas (2000): Empirische Sozialforschung: Grundlagen, Methoden, Anwendungen. Reinbeck: Rowohlt Taschenbuch Verlag.

Dixon-Fyle, Kanyhama (1994): Prevention as the best solution. In: Refugees, II, 22-25.

Duany, Wal and Duany, Julia (2000): Genesis of the Crisis in the Sudan. In: Spaulding J. and Beswick, S. (eds.): White Nile, Black Blood: War, Leadership, and Ethnicity from Khartoum to Kampala. Asmara: The Red Sea Press.

Dyson-Hudson, Rada and Dyson-Hudson, Neville (1980): Nomadic Pastoralism. In: Annual Review of Anthropology, 9, 15-61.

Eberwein, Wolf Dieter (2001): Humanitäre Hilfe, Flüchtlinge und Konfliktbearbeitung. Berlin: Papers.

Han, Petrus (2000): Soziologie der Migration: Erklärungsmodelle, Fakten, Politische Konsequenzen, Perspektiven. Stuttgart: Lucius und Lucius.

Hantingford, G.W.B. (1953): The Northern Nilo-Hamites. London: International African Institute.

Harir, Sharif (1994): Recycling the Past in the Sudan. In: Harir, Sharif and Tvedt, Terje (eds.): Short-Cut to Decay: The Case of the Sudan. Uppsala: Motala Grafiska.

Harrell Bond, Barbara (1999): The experience of refugees as recipients of aid. In: Ager, A. (ed.): Refugees: Perspectives on the Experience of Forced Migration. GB: Biddles Ltd.

Harrell-Bond, Barbara (2002): Can Humanitarian Work with Refugees be Humane? In: Human Rights Quarterly, 24, 51-85.

Harrell-Bond (2004): Response to Kibreab: Weapons of the Weak. In: Journal of Refugee Studies, 17 (1), 27-28.

Harrell-Bond, Barbara and Leopold, Mark (1994): An Overview of the World Refugee Crisis. In: Marsella, A. J., Bornemann, T. et al (eds.): Amidst Peril and Pain: The Mental Health and Well-Being of the World's Refugees. Washington: American Psychological Association.

Harrell-Bond, Barbara and Voutira, Eftihia (1995): In Search of the Locus of Trust: The Social World of the Refugee Camp. In: Daniel, E. V. and Knudsen, J. C. (eds.): Mistrusting Refugees. Berkeley et al: University of California Press.

Harrell-Bond, Barbara, Voutira, Eftihia et al (1992): Counting the Refugees: Gifts, Givers, Patrons and Clients. In: Journal of Refugee Studies, 5 (3-4), 205-225.

Human Rights Watch (2004): Sudan, Oil, and Human Rights. Brussels: Human Rights Watch.

Human Rights Watch (1990): "Denying the Honor of Living": Sudan: A Human Rights Disaster. New York et al: Human Rights Watch.

Hutchinson, Sharon E. (1996): Nuer Dilemmas: Coping with Money, War, and the State. Berkeley et al: University of California Press.

Ismael, Ellen (2005): Bukra, Insha' Allah: A look into Sudanese Culture. Bendestorf: Verlag Ellen Ismail-Schmidt.

Iten, Oswald (1977): Schwarzer Sudan: Die Stämme der Nuba, Schilluk, Dinka, Nuer, Azande und Latuka. Kreuzlingen: Neptun Verlag.

Iten, Oswald (1995): Zwischen allen Welten: Völker am Rande der Zivilisation. Zürich: Verlag Neue Zürcher Zeitung.

Johnson, Douglas H. (1994): Destruction and Reconstruction in the Economy of the Southern Sudan. In: Harir, Sharif and Tvedt, Terje (eds.): Short-Cut to Decay: The Case of the Sudan. Uppsala: Motala Grafiska.

Johnson, Douglas H. (1996): Increasing the Trauma of Return: An Assessment of the UN's Emergency Response to the Evacuation of the Sudanese Refugee Camps in Ethiopia, 1991. In: Tim Allen (ed.): In Search of Cool Ground: War, Flight and Homecoming in Northeast Arfrica. London: James Currey.

Johnson, Douglas H. (2004): The Root Causes of Sudan's Civil Wars. The international African Institute. Oxford: James Currey.

Jok, Madut Jok and Hutchinson, Sharon Elaine (1999): Sudan's Prolonged Second Civil War and The Militarization of Nuer and Dinka Ethnic Identities. In: African Studies Review, 42 (2), 125-145.

Kabera, John B. (1987): The Refugee Problem in Uganda. In: Rogge, J.R.: A third world dilemma. Totowa: Rowman and Littlefield.

Khalid, Mansour (1990): The Government They Deserve: the Role of the Elite in Sudan's Political Evolution. London, New York: Kegan Paul International Limited.

Khasiani, S.A. (1990): Refugee Research in Africa: Problems and Possibilities. In: International Migration Review, 28 (1), 369-376.

Kibreab, Gaim (2004): Pulling the Wool over the Eyes of the Strangers: Refugee Deceit and Trickery in Institutionalized Settings. In: Journal of Refugee Studies, 17 (1), 1-26.

Koehn, Peter H. (1995): Refugee Settlement and Repatriation in Africa: Development Prospects and Constraints. In: Adelman, H. and Sorenson, J. (eds.): African Refugees: Development Aid and Repatriation. Boulder et al: Westview Press.

Koser, Khalid (1993): Repatriation and information: a theoretical model. In: Black, R. and Robinson, V. (eds.): Geography and Refugees: Patterns and processes of change. London: Belhaven Press.

Kourula, Pirkko (1997): Broadening the Edges: Refugee Definition and International Protection Revisited. The Hague et al: Martinus Nijhoff Publishers.

Krieger, Mark (1999): Menschenrechte in arabo-islamischen Staaten: Am Beispiel Ägypten und Sudan. Frankfurt a. M.: Peter Lang GmbH.

Kromrey, Helmut (1998): Empirische Sozialforschung: Modelle und Methoden der Datenerhebung und Datenauswertung. Opladen: Leske + Budrich.

Kromrey, Helmut (2006): Empirische Sozialforschung. Stuttgart: UTB.

Kumar, Krishna (ed.) (1997): The Nature and Focus of International Assistance for Rebuilding War-Torn Societies: In: Rebuilding Societies After Civil War: Critical Roles for International Assistance. Boulder, London: Lynne Rienner Publishers.

Lado, Cleophas (1988): A note on 'traditional' agricultural land use: A case study from Maridi District, Southern Sudan. In: Malaysian Journal of Geography, 18, 25-34.

Lesch, Ann Mosely (1998): The Sudan: Contested National Identities. Bloomington: Indiana University Press. Oxford: James Currey Ltd.

Lesch, Ann Mosely (1999): Sudan: The Torn Country. In: Current History, 98 (628), 218-222.

Loescher, Gil (1992): Refugee Movements and International Security. The International Institute for Strategic Studies. London: Brassey's.

Marsella, Anthony J., Bornemann, Thomas et al (eds.) (1994): Introduction. In: Amidst Peril and Pain: The Mental Health and Well-Being of the World's Refugees. Washington: American Psychological Association.

Mayring, Philip (1990): Einführung in die qualitative Sozialforschung: Eine Anleitung zum qualitativen Denken. München: Psychologie Verlags Union.

Mayring, Philip (1993): Einführung in die qualitative Sozialforschung. Weinheim: Beltz.

Mayring, Phillip (2003): Qualitative Inhaltsanalyse: Grundlagen und Techniken. Weinheim: Beltz.

Merkx, Jozef (2002): Refugee identities and relief in an african borderland: a study of northern Uganda and southern Sudan. In: Refugee Survey Quarterly 21 (1/2), 113-146.

Moro, Leben Nelson (2004): Interethnic Relations in Exile: The Politics of Ethnicity among Sudanese Refugees in Uganda and Egypt. In: Journal of Refugee Studies, 17 (4), 420–436.

Moszynski, Peter (2005): Sudan: Peace at a snail's pace. In: Middle East International, 750, 17-18.

Nyaba, P.A. (1997): The Politics of Liberation in South Sudan: An Insider's View. Kampala: Fountain Publishers Ltd.

Ofcansky, Thomas (2000): Warfare and Instability Along the Sudan-Uganda Border: A Look at the Twentieth Century. In: Spaulding J. and Beswick, S. (eds.): White Nile, Black Blood: War, Leadership, and Ethnicity from Khartoum to Kampala. Asmara: The Red Sea Press.

Okello-Oloya, J.C. (1972): Acholi Customs. In: Uganda Journal, 36, 49-56.

Payne, Linda (1998): Rebuilding Communities in a Refugee Settlement: A Casebook from Uganda. Oxford: Oxfam Publications.

Petterson, Don (2003): Inside Sudan: Political Islam, Conflict, and Catastrophe: Revised and Updated. Boulder, Oxford: Westview Press.

Prunier, Gérard (2004): Rebel Movements and Proxy Warfare: Uganda, Sudan and the Congo (1986-99). In: African Affairs, 103 (412), p. 359-383.

Rogge, John R. (1994): Repatriation of refugees: A not so simple 'optimum' solution. In: Allen, T. and Morsink H. (eds.): When Refugees Go Home. Trenton: Africa World Press.

Rogge, John R. and Akol, Joshua O. (1989): Repatriation: Its Role in Resolving Africa's Refugee Dilemma. In: International Migration Review, 23 (2), p. 184-220.

Ryle, John (1982): Krieger des Weißen Nils: Die Dinka. Amsterdam: Time-Life Books.

Saldern, Matthias von (1998): Befragung und Beobachtung im Betrieb. Baltmannsweiler: Schneider Verlag Hohengehren.

Schäfers, Bernhard (ed.) (1998): Grundbegriffe der Soziologie. Opladen: Leske und Budrich.

Schimmel, Annemarie (1990): Die Religion des Islam: Eine Einführung. Stuttgart: Reclam.

Schmidinger, Thomas (2006): Der Sudan zwischen autoritärer Militärdiktatur und Staatszerfall. In: Österreichische Zeitschrift für Politikwissenschaft, 35, 189-205.

Sepulveda, Danielle C. (1995): Challenging the assumptions of repatriation. In: The Courier, 150, 83-85.

Seligman, Charles G. and Seligman Brenda Z. (1965): Pagan tribes of the Nilotic Sudan. London: Routledge & Kegan Paul.

Shiroya, O.J.E. (1972): The Lugbarra of Northwestern Uganda: Migration and early settlement. In: Uganda journal, 36, 23-34.

Simone, T. Abdou Maliqalim (1994): In Whose Image? Political Islam and Urban Practices in Sudan. Chicago, London: The University of Chicago Press.

Spaulding, Jay and Beswick, Stephanie (eds.) (2000): White Nile Black Blood: Historical Perspectives on Africa's longest Civil War and the Forced Transfer of Southern Sudanese Wealth to Khartoum (1820-1994). In: White Nile Black Blood: War, Leadership and Ethnicity from Khartoum to Kampala. Asmara: The Red Sea Press.

Stein, Barry N. (1986): Durable Solutions for Developing Country Refugees. In: International Migration Review, 20, 264-282.

Strauss, Anselm and Corbin, Juliet (1990): Basics of Qualitative Research: Grounded Theory Procedures and Techniques. Newbury Park et al: Sage Publications.

Strauss, Anselm and Corbin, Juliet (1996): Grounded Theory: Grundlagen Qualitativer Sozialforschung. Weinheim: Beltz.

Strübling, Jörg (2004): Grounded Theory: Zur sozialtheoretischen und epistemologischen Fundierung des Verfahrens der empirisch begründeten Theoriebildung. Wiesbaden: VS Verlag für Sozialwissenschaften.

Tetzlaff, Rainer (1992): Sudan: Selbstzerfleischung eines rassisch zweigeteilten Landes. In: Hofmeiner, R. and Matthies, V. (eds.): Vergessene Kriege in Afrika. Göttingen: Lamuv.

Treibel, Annette (1990): Migration in modernen Gesellschaften: Soziale Folgen von Einwanderung und Gastarbeit. Weinheim, München: Juventa Verlag.

Tucker, Archibald N. (1935): Survey of the Language Groups in the Southern Sudan. In: Bulletin of the School of Oriental Studies, 7(4), p. 861-896.

Tvedt, Terje (1994): The Collapse of the State in Southern Sudan After the Addis Ababa Agreement: A Study of Internal Causes and the Role of the NGOs. In: Harir, S. and Tvedt, T. (eds.): Short-Cut to Decay: The Case of the Sudan. Uppsala: Nordiska Afrikainstitutet.

UNHCR (1997): The State of the World's Refugees: A Humanitarian Agenda. Oxford: Oxford University Press.

Warner, Daniel (1994): Voluntary Repatriation and the Meaning of Return to Home: A Critique of Liberal Mathematics. In: Journal of Refugee Studies, 7, 160-174.

Woodward, Peter (1988): Uganda and Southern Sudan: peripheral politics and neighbour relations. In: Hansen, H. B. and Twaddle, M. (eds.): Uganda Now: Between Decay & Development. London et al: James Currey et al.

Young, John (2005): John Garang's Legacy to the Peace Process, the SPLM/A & the South. In: Review of African Political Economy, 32 (106), 535-548.

Zieck, Marjoleine (1997): UNHCR and Voluntary Repatriation of Refugees: A Legal Analysis. The Hague et al: Martinus Nijhoff Publishers.

Internet Sources

Augda, Oluwadare (1973): Arabism and Pan-Arabism in Sudanese Politics. In: The Journal of Modern African Studies, 11 (2), 177-200. URL: http://links/jstor.org/sici?sici=0022-278X%28197306%2911%3A2%3C177%3AAAPISP%362.0.CO%3B2-2 [date of access: 10.09.2005]

BMZ (2004): Migration in und aus Afrika. URL: www.bmz.de [date of access: 06.03.2005]

Gordon, Sophie, Vandewint, Carry et al. (2007): Reluctant Hosts: The Impact of the Lord's Resistance Army on Communities in Western Equatoria State, Southern Sudan. URL: http://www.worldvision.org/resources.nsf/main/LRA_report_200706.pdf/$file/LRA_report_200706.pdf?open&lid=LRA_pdf&lpos=day:txt:reluctant_hosts [date of access: 01.06.2007]

GoS and SPLA (2005): Comprehensive Peace Agreement. URL: http://www.unmis.org/English/documents/cpa-en.pdf [date of access: 10.09.2005]

Human Rights Watch (2006): Sudan's comprehensive peace agreement: The long road ahead. Africa Report No 106 – 31 March 2006. URL: http://www.reliefweb.int/library/documents/ 2006/icg-sdn-31mar.pdf [date of access: 01.04.2006]

IMU OCHA (2005): Sudan Transition and Recovery Database: Yei County, Version 3, July 2005. URL: http://www.unsudanig.org/ STAR-BASE/reports/Regional-reports/South/Equatoria/Yei.pdf [date of access: 03.03.2005]

IRIN News (2003): IRIN Webspecial on the Sudan Peace Process. URL: http://www.irinnews.org/webspecials/sudan/sudanp1.asp [date of access: 09.01.2006]

IRIN News (28.03.2006): SUDAN: Refugees urged to return home from Uganda. URL: http://www.irinnews.org/report.asp?ReportID=52467&SelectRegion=East_Africa&SelectCountry=SUDAN [date of access: 30.03.2006]

IRIN News (30.03.2006): War-related deaths in the North very high – report. URL: http://www.irinnews.org/report.asp?ReportID=52512 & SelectRegion=East_Africa&SelectCountry=UGANDA [date of access: 01.04.2006]

IRIN News (20.06.2007): EAST AFRICA: Accelerating the return of Sudanese refugees. URL: http://www.irinnews.org/Report.aspx?ReportId=72839 [date of access: 20.06.2007]

IRIN News (25.06.2007): Repair infrastructure so that the displaced can return home – IOM: URL: http://www.irinnews.org/Report.aspx?ReportId=72905 [date of access: 26.06.2007]

Mayring, Philipp (2000): Qualitative Content Analysis [28 paragraphs]. Forum: Qualitative Social Research [Online Journal], 1(2). URL: http://www.qualitative-research.net/fqs-texte/2-00/2-00mayring-e.htm [date of access: 02.01.2006]

Öhm, Mafred (2006): Sudan: Politischer Übergang ohne Machtwechsel. URL: http://library.fes.de/pdf-files/id/03887a.pdf [date of access: 15.05.2007]

Terlinden, Ulf (2004): IGAD: Papiertiger vor Mammutaufgaben. URL: http://library.fes.de/pdf-files/iez/01847.pdf [date of access: 15.05.2007]

UNHCR (2006): South Sudan: UNHCR Global Appeal 2006. URL: http://www.unhcr.org/cgi-bin/texis/vtx/home/opendoc.pdf?tbl=PU &id=43706f020 [date of access: 02.04.2006]

UNHCR (27.03.2006): Return home now possible for South Sudan's refugees in Uganda. URL: http://www.unhcr.org/cgi-bin/texis/vtx/news/opendoc.htm?tbl=NEWS&id=442811b54 [date of access: 29.03.2006]

UNHCR (03.04.2006): On International Mine Awareness Day, UNHCR concerned over dangers facing returning refugees to South Sudan. URL: http://www.unhcr.org/cgi-bin/texis/vtx/news/ opendoc.htm?tbl=NEWS&id=44315a584 [date of access: 04.04.2006]

UN News Service (18.05.2007): Number of returning Southern Sudanese refugees tops 140,000 – UN agencies. URL: http://www.un.org/apps/news/story.asp?NewsID=22600&Cr=Southern&Cr1=sudan# [date of access: 03.06.2007]

Unpublished documents

DED (2005): Arua Refugee Programme: Rhino Camp / Imvepi / Madi Okollo: Project Proposal – 2005.

DED (2005)a: Refugee popn.statistics, in OK, RH and IM settlements by end of March 2005.

Education Section Rhino Camp Settlement (2005): Monthly report for April 2005.

Appendix

1. **Name**
2. **Age**
3. **Place of birth**
4. **Ethnic background**

5. **Life in the Sudan before the war**

   a) Where did you live? Which county is that?
   b) How did you like your life then?
   c) Have your parents been able to provide education for you? Up to which level?
   d) Before you left, what have you been doing there?

6. **Life in the Sudan during the war**

   a) When did the conflict start to affect your area?
   b) Who do you think is responsible for the war?
   c) Can you please describe to me, how life was for you during those days?
   d) Who has mainly disturbed you?

7. **Departure and flight**

   a) When did you leave the area? (Time between effects and departure) When the country? Why not earlier (maybe even before the war reached you)? What held you back?
   b) How did you feel, once it had become clear that you would leave your home?
   c) How did you prepare your departure? What did you take with you?
   d) Did you flee to a different place before coming to Uganda? Where to? How long did you stay over there? Why did you leave again?
   e) Which stations did you take from fleeing your home up to settling at Rhino Camp?
   f) How did this constant movement make you feel?

8. **Life inside the Rhino Camp Settlement**

   a) What do you like about life inside the settlement?
   b) Are your children going to school? Which kind?
   c) Do you inform yourself about the current conditions in Sudan and your home area? By which means?

9. Repatriation plans

a) What are your wishes for your repatriation? When and why?
b) Where do you want to go to?
c) Do you still have a plot over there? Any properties on it? Is somebody over there protecting your plot against occupation? Are you sure to still receive it?
d) Did anyone of your family already go back to start creating a new place?
e) Do you consider it secure over there?

10. Expectations of the future

a) What do you think needs to be done so that Sudan can provide better living conditions for you? Who should do that?
b) Do you expect to receive any help for getting settled and building up your livelihood? From whom and how?
c) How do you think the people who did not flee the country will receive you and the other returnees when you reach home?
d) Do you expect the peace agreement to be the final one?
e) Do you expect any further civil war within South? How do you think war can be prevented?
f) How do you feel towards the SPLA?
g) How do you feel towards the Sudanese government?
h) What is your personal opinion about the possibility of independence for Southern Sudan and its consequences?

11. Anything to add?

Dear Respondent, this is a purely academic research about the repatriation of Southen Sudanese Refugees. Your responses will be treated highly confidential. As no names are mentioned, none of your answers can be linked to you as a person. Thus, the researcher kindly asks you to feel free to respond in an open and honest way. Thank you very much for your effort to make this research a success.

I. Background information

1. How old are you? ________ Of which gender are you? ☐ male☐ female
2. Where did you live before you had to flee? ____________________________

   (town or village / county)
3. In which year did you leave your home? ____________________________
4. In which year did you arrive at Rhino Camp? ____________________________
5. What were your reasons for fleeing your home?

____

____

____

____

____

II. Repatriation

The repatriation of refugees will be voluntary, meaning that refugees can decide themselves at what particular time they want to return to Sudan. If they wish so, they can remain in Uganda up to several years.

With this information in your mind:

1. Do you wish to leave Uganda as soon as possible or remain over here for some time?

☐ leave as soon as possible

☐ remain for some time → For how long? ________

Please explain, why you wish to leave at this particular time.

____

____

____

____

____

2. Where are you planning to return to?

________________________________ (town or village / county)

III. Future in Sudan

1. Since you became a refugee, did you ever go back to Sudan?

☐ **yes, last time in** _______________ (month / year) ☐ **no**

2. Did you or any other family member start to reconstruct your place in Sudan already?

☐ **yes, we started in** _______________ (month / year) **[go to a]** ☐ **no [go to 3.]**

a) Who went back to your home to start the reconstruction and how do you organize for it?

____

____

____

3. Do you consider the area of your home as secure?

☐ **yes** ☐ **no** ☐ **uncertain**

Please explain your reasons for this consideration.

____

____

____

4. Do you expect the peace between North and South Sudan to last from now on?

☐ **yes** ☐ **no** ☐ **uncertain**

Please explain your reasons for this consideration.

____

____

____

____

5. Do you expect any conflicts within South Sudan in the future? (i.e. tribal or political conflicts)

☐ **yes** ☐ **no** ☐ **uncertain**

Please explain your reasons for this consideration.

____

____

____

____

6. Do you wish for South Sudan to seperate from North Sudan in the future?

☐ **yes - become independent** ☐ **no - remain united** ☐ **uncertain**

Please explain your reasons for this consideration.

____

____

____

____

Thank you very much for your assistance!

Spektrum
Berliner Reihe zu Gesellschaft, Wirtschaft und Politik in Entwicklungsländern
hrsg. von PD Dr. Dr. Ulrich van der Heyden, Prof. Dr. Volker Lühr, Dr. Ulrike Schultz und Prof. Dr. Manfred Schulz
(Freie Universität Berlin)

Verda Kaya
Lehmburgen und Wellblechdächer
Architektur und Lebensform bei den Dagara in Ghana
"We shape our buildings, thereafter they shape us" – dieses Zitat von Winston Churchill stellt die Ethnologin Verda Kaya ihrer Arbeit voran, in der sie die Wechselwirkung zwischen Architektur und Lebensform bei den Dagara in Ghana analysiert. Das Haus wird als Konsumobjekt aufgefaßt, das verschiedene Lebensstile reflektiert und nicht nur Auskunft über seine Bewohner, sondern auch über gesellschaftliche Transformationsprozesse gibt. Ausgangspunkt der Betrachtung sind Missionierung und Kolonialisierung, die mit ihren Prozessen der Urbanisierung, sozialen Differenzierungen und der Elitenbildung zur Entstehung neuer Architekturformen beigetragen haben. Anhand von Wohnbiographien, zahlreichen Interviews, Fotos und Grundrissen verschiedener Dagara Häuser wird dargestellt, wie der Übergang von „traditioneller" Architektur zu „modernen" Bauweisen und -formen veränderte Wertvorstellungen und Bedürfnisse widerspiegelt.
Bd. 70, 2002, 176 S., 17,90 €, br., ISBN 3-8258-4760-8

Rita Schäfer
Gender und ländliche Entwicklung in Afrika
Eine kommentierte Bibliographie
Diese kommentierte Bibliographie bietet einen umfassenden Überblick über den Forschungsstand zur Frauen- und Geschlechterforschung in ländlichen Gebieten Afrikas. Die Zusammenstellung basiert auf der Auswertung von über 100 ethnologischen, soziologischen, agrarwissenschaftlichen und entwicklungspolitischen Fachzeitschriften. Darüber hinaus wurden zahlreiche Monographien und Sammelbände integriert. Einzigartig ist die Dokumentation der veröffentlichten und unveröffentlichten Beiträge afrikanischer Wissenschaftlerinnen und Entwicklungsexpertinnen zur Thematik. Indem diese Bibliographie europäische, amerikanische und afrikanische Literatur einbezieht, informiert sie mit über 1500 Titeln und Kommentaren in umfassender Weise über Forschungserkenntnisse unterschiedlicher Fachgebiete und Erfahrungen aus Entwicklungsprojekten. Mit ihrer interdisziplinären Perspektive richtet sie sich an Wissenschaftler/-innen, Studierende und Mitarbeiter/-innen in der Entwicklungszusammenarbeit.
Bd. 75, 2., aktualis. u. erw. Aufl. 2003, 472 S., 30,90 €, br., ISBN 3-8258-5053-6

David William Cohen;
E. S. Atieno Odhiambo
Wer begräbt SM?
Politik des Wissens und Soziologie der Macht in Afrika. Aus dem Amerikanischen von Sibylle Alsayad und Adelheid Seyler. Vorwort zur deutschen Ausgabe von Georg Elwert
"Fünf Monate kämpften die Parteien vor Gericht. Spannend schildern Cohen und Odhiambo, wie der Konflikt die kenianische Nation entzweite, wie von Luo aus Dörfern über die städtische Intelligenz und Oberschüler bis hin zum Präsidenten Partei bezogen wurde. Nur der historische Luo-Repräsentant und Führer der Opposition Oginga Odinga hielt sich zurück. Es ging um den Ort eines Begräbnisses. Wo soll der bekannte Anwalt S. M. Otieno begraben werden? In der Stadt, wie seine Frau unter Berufung auf das moderne Leben und den Verstorbenen forderte, oder in der Heimat, wie der Bruder unter Berufung auf Tradition und ebenfalls auf den Verstorbenen einklagte. Dies mittlerweile klassische Werk ist etwas anderes als eine ethnographische Gerichtsberichterstattung. Beispielgebend wird hier analysiert, wie aus variierenden und zum Teil inkonsistenten Einzelinformationen und systematische

LIT Verlag Berlin – Hamburg – London – Münster – Wien – Zürich
Fresnostr. 2 48159 Münster
Tel.: 0251 / 620 32 22 – Fax: 0251 / 922 60 99
e-Mail: vertrieb@lit-verlag.de – http://www.lit-verlag.de

Ausblendung anderer Wissensbestände parteiische Diskurse geformt werden, wie sie in ihrer Resonanz getestet werden, wie sie bei anderen populären Diskursen Themen, stilistische Figuren und Referenzen – bis hin zum allgegenwärtigen Shakespeare – entlehnen und für diese wieder zu einer Referenz werden. ... Dieses Buch wird gefeiert als Paradigma postmoderner Vielstimmigkeit. ... "
(Aus dem Vorwort)
Bd. 76, 2001, 208 S., 15,90 €, br.,
ISBN 3-8258-5076-5

Stefanie Krug
Anthropologie der Kriegs- und Nachkriegszeit in Äthiopien
"Heldenhafter Kämpfer nannten sie dich – Wie heißt Du jetzt?" TPLF (Ex)-Guerillakämpfer/-innen in Äthiopien
Die Arbeit beruht auf einer partizipativen Feldforschung in einem Reintegrationsprojekt demobilisierter TPLF *(Tigray People's Liberation Front)* Kämpfer/-innen. Die Nachkriegsproblematiken dieser Ex-Kämpfer/-innen, die in einem Alter zwischen 11 und 14 Jahren zur Guerilla kamen und dort ihr halbes Leben verbrachten, werden analysiert und eingebettet in eine Anthropologie des Krieges. Die Arbeit umfaßt zwei Hauptteile: Einerseits die Darstellung der aktuellen sozio-ökonomischen Lebenssituation, u. a. gender-spezifische Identitätsaspekte, Prozesse der Entideologisierung, traumatische Gewalterfahrungen sowie Fragen der Zugehörigkeit. Andererseits werden Institutionalisierungsprozesse und die Machtzentralisierung der TPLF kritisch beschrieben. Ergänzt und weiter verdichtet werden diese Analysen durch emische Perspektiven der ehemaligen Kämpfer/-innen. Mit diesen Innenansichten des Guerillakrieges soll die differente Lebensqualität aufgezeigt werden, die mit diesem sozialen Raum verbunden war und die kollektive Identitäten konstituierte, welche bis heute prägend auf diese Erinnerungsgemeinschaft wirkt.
Bd. 77, 2001, 210 S., 17,90 €, br.,
ISBN 3-8258-5089-7

Volkmar Blum
Hybridisierung von unten
Nation und Gesellschaft im mittleren Andenraum
Lateinamerika gilt als Paradigma kultureller Mischung. Die "kreolischen Pioniere" der Unabhängigkeit stehen für eine Überwindung der exklusiven, rassistischen oder völkischen Nationenkonzepte Europas und Nordamerikas. Eine historische Betrachtung verdeutlicht hingegen, daß die lateinamerikanischen Eliten auf der Grundlage des iberischen Protorassismus eine Vielzahl von Kategorien entwickelten, um "die Anderen" in vielfältigen Abstufungen gesondert zu behandeln. Den "wissenschaftlichen Rassismus" griffen sie begierig auf, um die Exklusion zu verschärfen. Dennoch setzte sich im andinen Raum mit der Mestizaje ein inklusives Nationenkonzept durch, das die Hegemonie einer mestizischen "Leitkultur" proklamierte. Hybridisierungsprozesse hingegen wurden von der "indianischen" Bevölkerung vorgetragen, die ihnen zugeschriebene exklusive Kategorien unterlief und zunehmend räumliche, soziale und kulturelle Grenzen durchbrach. Dies zeigt sich auf so unterschiedlichen Gebieten wie der Arbeitskultur, den Netzwerken sozialer Sicherung und den neuen indigenen Bewegungen. Nicht der kreolische Diskurs, sondern die handlungsgeleitete Hybridisierung der (ehemals) indianischen Bevölkerung prägte die Entwicklung von Nation und Gesellschaft im Andenraum.
Bd. 79, 2001, 224 S., 19,90 €, br.,
ISBN 3-8258-5231-8

Ulrike Schuerkens
Transformationsprozesse in der Elfenbeinküste und in Ghana
Eine historisch-vergleichende Analyse des Verhältnisses von Lebensgeschichten und strukturellen Wandlungsprozessen
Alltagsthemen werden selten von Forschem thematisiert. Der Verlauf des Arbeitslebens im modernen Afrika gehört zu diesen wenig behandelten Gebieten. Mit diesem Buch stellt die Autorin ihre Forschungen zum Bereich der Transformation des Arbeitssystems in

der Elfenbeinküste und in Ghana vor. Diese Forschungen beruhen auf intensiver Feldforschung vor allem in urbanen Zentren, aber auch in ländlichen Gegenden. In dieser Studie wird der soziale Wandel des Arbeitssystems anhand von strukturellen Transformationsprozessen und Lebensgeschichten betagter Männer erforscht. Diese komparative Untersuchung kann zeigen, welche Art von Symbiose sich durch die Konfrontation von unterschiedlichen Sozialsystemen (autochthone Gruppen und koloniale bzw. neokoloniale Staaten) herauskristallisiert hat. Die vorliegenden Forschungsergebnisse sind kumulativer Art, da sie auf Globalisierunsprozesse hinweisen die in vielen Bereichen, die die Soziologie und die Anthropologie untersuchen, vonstatten gehen. Sie weisen auf Restrukturierungen hin, die sei; den vierziger und fünfziger Jahren des 20. Jahrhunderts westafrikanische Länder verändert haben. Durch diese Transformationsprozesse werden lokale Gesellschaften an globale Dimensionen gebunden. Das Paradigma der Entwicklung ermöglicht es, den Akzent auf die Interaktion zweier unterschiedlicher Sozialsysteme zu legen, auf Mischungen, auf Fusionen und auf die Einbettung in eine Geschichte, die mehr und mehr durch ein Weltsystem geprägt wird.
Bd. 80, 2001, 320 S., 25,90 €, br.,
ISBN 3-8258-4770-5

Sabine Herzog
Das Matriarchat als geschlechtssymmetrische Gesellschaftsform?
Die Khasi von Meghalaya/Indien
Der Überblick über Entstehung und Verlauf des bereits seit 150 Jahren andauernden Matriarchatsdiskurses verdeutlicht die Problematik, die sich aus der Zuschreibung des Geschlechterverhältnisses in matriarchal organisierten Gesellscharten ergibt. In der vorliegenden Arbeit wird die Hypothese einer Geschlechtssymmetrie in Matriarchaten am Beispiel der im Nordosten Indiens lebenden Khasi aufgestellt. Nach der Darstellung ihres Gesellschaftssystems werden die Einflußbereiche von Frauen und Männern in verschiedenen Machtfeldem analysiert und auf eine Balance der Geschlechter hin überprüft.
Bd. 81, 2001, 112 S., 17,90 €, br.,
ISBN 3-8258-5404-3

Doreen Montag
Gesundheit und Krankheit im Urubamba-Tal/Peru
Die emische Kategorisierung von Krankheit als Determinante der Heilerwahl und Vermittler zwischen traditioneller und Biomedizin
Urubamba liegt im heiligen Tal der Incas, am Ostabhang der Anden. Seine Bewohner haben Zugang zur traditionellen und Biomedizin. Das vielfältige Angebot an medizinischen Leistungen prägt die Inanspruchnahme im Krankheitsfall eines Urubambinos. Die Wahl des adäquaten Heilers eines bestimmten Deutungsmusters ist theoretisch konfliktverbunden. Wie gehen die Urubambinos damit um? Gibt es für Sie eine Trennung zwischen der traditionellen und der Biomedizin? In diesem Buch wird die theoretische Darstellung einer Konfliktbildung bei der Auswahl unterschiedlicher Heilsysteme dem aktuellen Umgang der Urubambinos mit dem Aspekt Krankheit gegenübergestellt. Die Akteursgruppen der Patienten, traditionellen Heiler und Ärzte und ihre emische Kategorisierung von Krankheit und Gesundheit stehen dabei im Vordergrund.
Bd. 82, 2002, 136 S., 15,90 €, br.,
ISBN 3-8258-5701-8